peer learning

in higher education

learning from & with each other

EDITED BY **DAVID BOUD, RUTH COHEN & JANE SAMPSON**

KOGAN PAGE

Dedication

In memory of Geoff Anderson, our collaborator, who did not live to see the fruits of our projects.

First published in 2001

Kogan Page Limited
120 Pentonville Road
London N1 9JN
UK

Stylus Publishing Inc
22883 Quicksilver Drive
Sterling VA 20166-2012
USA

© David Boud, Ruth Cohen, Jane Sampson and individual contributors

British Library Cataloguing in Publication Data

A CIP record for this book is available from the British Library.

ISBN 0 7494 3612 3

Typeset by JS Typesetting, Wellingborough, Northants

Contents

Contributors

David Boud is Professor of Adult Education, Faculty of Education, University of Technology, Sydney (UTS).

Ruth Cohen is former Head of the School of Adult Education, Faculty of Education, UTS.

Jim Cooper is Senior Lecturer in the Faculty of Law, UTS.

Robert Connor is a Lecturer in management, Faculty of Business, UTS.

Mark Freeman is an Associate Professor in finance and economics, Faculty of Business, UTS.

Ray Gordon is a Lecturer in management in the Faculty of Business, UTS.

Denise Kirkpatrick is Professor and Director of the Teaching and Learning Centre, University of New England.

Brian Lederer is a Lecturer in the Faculty of Information Technology, UTS.

Jo McKenzie is Senior Lecturer in the Institute for Interactive Multimedia and Learning, UTS.

Robert McLaughlan is Senior Lecturer in the National Centre for Groundwater Management, UTS.

Richard Raban is Head of the Department of Software Engineering, Faculty of Information Technology, UTS.

Jane Sampson is a Lecturer in adult education, Faculty of Education, UTS.

Jenny Toynbee Wilson is Associate Professor in Visual Communication, Faculty of Design, Architecture and Building, UTS.

Acknowledgements

Funding for the projects that led to the production of this book was provided through National Teaching Development Grants by the Commonwealth Committee on University Teaching and Staff Development, Canberra.

Chapter 5 is drawn from Boud, D, Cohen, R and Sampson, J (1999). Peer learning and assessment, *Assessment and Evaluation in Higher Education*, **24** (4), pp 413–26.

1

Introduction: making the move to peer learning

David Boud

In everyday life we continually learn from each other. For most of the things we need in our working and personal lives we find enough information and guidance from friends and colleagues. It is relatively uncommon to take a course or consult a teacher. We draw upon whatever resources we need wherever we can find them. Most people who use word-processing packages have not studied them formally: they receive tips from others, observe what they do and ask questions. Similarly, when buying a car, reviews in newspapers or magazines might be read, owners of cars of the type wanted consulted and sales staff listened to.

It might be argued that these are not necessarily the most efficient ways to go about learning and that they do not always lead to us obtaining accurate information, but they do meet the needs of most people in a timely and convenient fashion. The advantage in learning from people we know is that they are, or have been, in a similar position to ourselves. They have faced the same challenges as we have in the same context, they talk to us in our own language and we can ask them what may appear, in other situations, to be silly questions.

Learning from each other is not only a feature of informal learning, it occurs in all courses at all levels. Students have conversations about what they are learning inside and outside classrooms whether teachers are aware of it or not. The first approach, when stuck on a problem, is normally to ask another student, not the teacher. Not only can they provide each other with useful information but sharing the experience of learning also makes it less burdensome and more enjoyable. The power of peer learning is manifest daily in popular culture and many books and movies illustrate its influence. *The*

Paper Chase is a classic example of a feature film that portrays students learning from each other in competitive professional courses.

As teachers, we often fool ourselves in thinking that what we do is necessarily more important for student learning than other activities in which they engage. Our role is vital. However, if we place ourselves in the position of mediating all that students need to know, we not only create unrealistic expectations but we potentially deskill students by preventing them from developing the vital skills of effectively learning from each other needed in life and work. The skill of obtaining accurate information is not learned by being given accurate information by a teacher but through practice in discerning how to judge the accuracy of the information we receive.

This book is based on the assumption that there is considerable benefit in taking what we know of the value of informal peer learning, making it explicit and using it more directly in the design and conduct of higher education courses. Formalizing the informal is not intended to give teachers a more prominent or controlling role in informal learning, but to realize the potential benefits of peer learning so that all students can benefit from it, not just those who are socially adept or best networked. It is neither possible nor desirable to formalize all aspects of peer learning. However, quite modest moves in that direction can have a large impact on learning compared to the effort expended by teachers.

The book is also based on the premise that peer learning – that is, learning with and from each other – is a necessary and important aspect of all courses. The role it plays varies widely and the forms it takes are very diverse, but without it students gain an impoverished education.

The aim of the book is to explore the use of peer learning in formal courses. It addresses questions such as:

● What is peer learning and what is it good for?
● How can it best be fostered?
● What issues need to be considered by teachers and students?

It draws on the direct experience of the authors in using peer learning in their own courses and in studying its effects. The focus is on higher education but many of the ideas are applicable more widely.

What is peer learning and why is it important?

Peer learning is not a single, undifferentiated educational strategy. It encompasses a broad sweep of activities. For example, researchers from the University of Ulster identified 10 different models of peer learning (Griffiths, Houston and Lazenbatt, 1995). These ranged from the traditional proctor model, in which senior students tutor junior students, to the more innovative learning cells, in which students in the same year form partnerships to assist each other with both course content and personal concerns. Other models involved discussion seminars, private study groups, parrainage (a buddy system) or counselling, peer-assessment schemes, collaborative project or laboratory work, projects in different sized (cascading) groups, workplace mentoring and community activities.

The term 'peer learning', however, remains abstract. The sense in which we use it here suggests a two-way, reciprocal learning activity. Peer learning should be mutually beneficial and involve the sharing of knowledge, ideas and experience between the participants. It can be described as a way of moving beyond independent to interdependent or mutual learning (Boud, 1988).

Students learn a great deal by explaining their ideas to others and by participating in activities in which they can learn from their peers. They develop skills in organizing and planning learning activities, working collaboratively with others, giving and receiving feedback and evaluating their own learning. Peer learning is becoming an increasingly important part of many courses, and it is being used in a variety of contexts and disciplines in many countries.

The potential of peer learning is starting to be realized, but examination of the ways in which it is used in existing courses suggests that practices are often introduced in an *ad hoc* way, without consideration of their implications. When such practices are used unsystematically, students unfamiliar with this approach become confused about what they are supposed to be doing, they miss opportunities for learning altogether, and fail to develop the skills expected of them. Much peer learning occurs informally without staff involvement, and students who are already effective learners tend to benefit disproportionately when it is left to chance.

Formalized peer learning can help students learn effectively. At a time when university resources are stretched and demands upon staff are increasing, it offers students the opportunity to learn from each other. It gives them considerably more practice than traditional teaching and learning methods in taking responsibility for their own learning and, more generally, learning how to learn. It is not a substitute for teaching and activities designed and conducted by staff members, but an important addition to the repertoire of teaching and learning activities that can enhance the quality of education.

It is important to consider who are the 'peers' in peer learning. Generally, peers are other people in a similar situation to each other who do not have a role in that situation as teacher or expert practitioner. They may have considerable experience and expertise or they may have relatively little. They share the status as fellow learners and they are accepted as such. Most importantly, they do not have power over each other by virtue of their position or responsibilities. Throughout the book we will be discussing the role of students who are in the same classes as those from whom they are learning.

Peer *teaching,* or peer *tutoring,* is a far more instrumental strategy in which advanced students, or those in later years, take on a limited instructional role. It often requires some form of credit or payment for the person acting as the teacher. Peer teaching is a well-established practice in many universities, whereas reciprocal peer learning is often considered to be incidental – a component of other more familiar strategies, such as the discussion group (see, for example, Brookfield and Preskill, 1999). As a consequence, until recently, reciprocal peer learning has not been identified as a phenomenon in its own right that might be used to students' advantage.

Reciprocal peer learning typically involves students within a given class or cohort. This makes peer learning relatively easy to organize because there are fewer timetabling problems. There is also no need to pay or reward with credit the more experienced students responsible for peer teaching. Students in reciprocal peer learning are by definition peers, and so there is less confusion about roles compared with situations in which one of the 'peers' is a senior student, or is in an advanced class, or has special expertise.

Reciprocal peer learning emphasizes students simultaneously learning and contributing to other students' learning. Such communication is based on mutual experience and so they are better able to make equal contributions. It more closely approximates to Habermas' notion of an 'ideal speech act' in which issues of power and domination are less prominent than when one party has a designated 'teaching' role and thus takes on a particular kind of authority for the duration of the activity.

We define peer learning in its broadest sense, then, as 'students learning from and with each other in both formal and informal ways'. The emphasis is on the learning process, including the emotional support that learners offer each other, as much as the learning task itself. In peer teaching the roles of teacher and learner are fixed, whereas in peer learning they are either undefined or may shift during the course of the learning experience. Staff may be actively involved as group facilitators or they may simply initiate student–directed activities such as workshops or learning partnerships.

According to Topping's review of literature, surprisingly little research has been done into either dyadic reciprocal peer tutoring or same-year group tutoring (Topping, 1996). He identified only 10 studies, all with a very narrow, empirical focus. This suggests that the teaching model, rather than the learning model, is still the most common way of understanding how students assist each other. Although the teaching model has value, we must also consider the learning process itself if we want to make the best use of peers as resources for learning.

As mentioned earlier, it is important to recognize that peer learning is not a single practice. It covers a wide range of different activities each of which can be combined with others in different ways to suit the needs of a particular course. It is like peer assessment in this regard (Falchikov, 2001) and it is unfortunately similarly misunderstood as referring to a particular practice.

Why do we need to focus now on peer learning?

There are both pragmatic reasons and reasons of principle for the current focus on peer learning in university courses. It would be naïve to ignore the most pressing pragmatic reason even though it has little to do with concerns about teaching and learning. It is that in many countries there is considerable pressure on university funding, which has lead to staff being required to teach more students without diminution in the quality of the student learning. This has prompted a search for teaching and learning strategies that might help staff to cope with larger student numbers without increasing their overall workload. Peer learning is promising because it appears to maintain or increase student learning with less input from staff.

We are not so cynical as to think that this has been the prime motive driving interest in peer learning. Concurrent with this financial pressure has been a reassessment of the goals of university courses and new emphasis has been placed on generic learning outcomes. Employers now want graduates who possess a broader range of skills and abilities to communicate effectively beyond their specialization, and so courses are now expected to develop in students what are variously termed transferable skills (Assiter, 1995), key competencies (Mayer, 1992), generic attributes (Wright, 1995) or capabilities (Stephenson and Yorke, 1998). These are part of a repertoire of skills and strategies designed to foster lifelong learning in the student. Candy, Crebert and O'Leary (1994: p. xii) cited 'peer-assisted and self-directed learning' as the first of five teaching methods in undergraduate courses that encourage graduates to become lifelong learners, as well as helping them to develop 'reflective practice and critical self-awareness'.

Technology is now an important driver towards the use of peer learning. Effective courses do not involve the delivery of substantial amounts of content through new media (Stephenson, 2001). Web-based activities appear to be most effective when there is direct interaction between staff and students and among students themselves. The nature of the Web as a medium means that it is impossible for a teacher to personally deal with a large number of interactions between a teacher and individual students. This soon becomes far more time consuming than any form of conventional teaching. How then is the need for interaction reconciled with the limitations on the capacity of teaching staff? Peer learning provides a key solution to this dilemma. It is possible for tutors to deal with the volume of interaction emerging from *groups* of students working together in a way that is not realistic with individuals.

In addition to these 'mainstream' motives, it is also argued that collective forms of peer learning suit some students better than the individualistic teaching and learning practices of traditional courses (Slavin, 1995; Chalmers and Volet, 1997). This has been particularly true for women and students from some cultural backgrounds, as peer learning activities value cooperation within groups above competition and encourages greater respect for the varied experiences and backgrounds of the participants.

How does peer learning link to other ideas and practices?

A common misconception is that peer learning is simply about using group work in courses. This is not surprising, as some of the strongest proponents of group work are also major scholars of cooperative learning (Johnson and Johnson, 1997). Of course group work does involve peers learning from each other (Jaques, 2000), but much peer learning also occurs on a one-to-one basis and peer learning need not be primarily about learning to work in groups.

There are a number of other practices discussed particularly in the North American literature, which have some similarities to peer learning. These include cooperative learning and collaborative learning. There is a substantial literature on cooperative learning (for example, Jacob, 1999) and it is discussed in best selling books, such as Johnson and Johnson (1997). However, most of the applications are not in higher education and the role of the teacher is much stronger than in the examples we will be discussing here.

Cooperative learning grew out of developmental psychology – cognitive, social, developmental psychology. Attention was focused on the processes of group interaction, individual skill development, social learning and management of the educational environment. These activities took place within an established body of knowledge/discipline and authority for knowledge was vested in the teacher. The emphasis was on the process used by teachers to achieve specified educational outcomes. Teacher intervention and management is expected to set goals, determine activities and measure and evaluate educational achievement. Group learning is structured to achieve a balance between process and skills and knowledge acquisition.

The practice known as collaborative learning is used more in higher education in the US. The emphasis is on the setting of open-ended but focused tasks to students who work together to solve them, thus encouraging interdependent learning (Bruffee, 1999). Collaborative learning had its genesis in adult and adolescent learning with the notion of participatory learning. Groups engage in exploration of ideas and knowledge and learning to learn. Teachers may set up structured activities but their specific means of achievement are left to the group. Learning is the key concept, not education. The teacher is more a facilitator, negotiating the learning and evaluation with learners and handing over more control. The group determines group roles and it is the personal sense of the learning that signifies collaborative learning. Critical thinking, problem solving, sensemaking and personal transformation, the social construction of knowledge – exploration, discussion, debate, criticism of ideas are the stuff of collaborative learning. The implicit assumption is that adult learners are experienced social beings who can act in a collaborative manner, organize themselves, have some intrinsic motivation or educationally imposed motivation and do not require the imposed structures of the facilitator to inspire learning. Bruffee (1999) names this approach 'constructive conversation' – an educative experience in which students learn by constructing knowledge as they talk together and reach consensus or dissent. Dissent, questioning each other's views within a group, is a necessary part of learning.

Despite these distinctions, there is considerable overlap in practice between cooperative and collaborative learning, and in some discussions the terms are used interchangeably. However, there tends to be a greater emphasis on direction by teachers in cooperative learning. There are also other approaches that have some common characteristics with these and include features of peer learning. An example is the use of syndicate groups, common in management education but used extensively in other settings (Collier, 1983).

What outcomes does peer learning aim to promote?

Peer learning promotes certain types of learning outcomes. Some of these are not so easily achieved through other teaching and learning strategies. While different varieties of peer learning emphasize different outcomes, some of the common learning outcomes include:

- *Working with others.* The skills involved in working with others include teamwork and being a member of a learning community. Peer learning can prompt a sense of responsibility for one's own and others' learning and development of increased confidence and self-esteem through engaging in a community of learning and learners. Much learning takes place from sharing others' experiences, existing knowledge and skills. Students learn to acknowledge the backgrounds and contributions of the people they are working with. Peer learning necessarily involves students working together to develop collaborative skills. Working together gives them practice in planning and teamwork and makes them part of a learning community in which they have a stake.
- *Critical enquiry and reflection.* Challenges to existing ways of thinking arise from more detailed interchanges between students in which points of view are argued and positions justified. It provides opportunities for formulating questions rather than simply responding to those posed by others. There is evidence to suggest that fostering critical reflection and reassessment of views more readily comes from interchange between peers (Smith and Hatton, 1993) than even from well-planned discussion sessions with teachers. Depending on the particular activities chosen, peer learning can provide opportunities for deep engagement in the learning process, as students are learning through their relationships with peers, not just trying to 'beat the system'. Students are often better able to reflect on and explore ideas when the presence and authority of a staff member (Boud and Walker, 1998) do not influence them. In peer learning contexts students generally communicate more about the subject area than they do when staff are present. They are able to articulate what they understand and to be more open to be critiqued by peers, as well as learning from listening to and critiquing others.
- *Communication and articulation of knowledge, understanding and skills.* Concept development often occurs through the testing of ideas on others and the rehearsing of positions that enable learners to express their under-standing of ideas and concepts. It is often only when they are expressed

and challenged that students appreciate whether they have a good grasp of what they are studying. There are often limited opportunities for this without peer learning activities. Invaluable additional practice in practising skills is often available in peer settings especially when direct supervision is not required for safety or ethical reasons.

- *Managing learning and how to learn.* Peer learning activities require students to develop self-management skills and managing with others. They are not being continually prompted by deadlines from staff (although there may be some ultimate deadlines) but through the exigencies of cooperating with others. This demands different kinds of self-responsibility as it involves obligations to others and maintaining one's position in a peer group. Many peer-learning activities require students to cooperate on quite substantial tasks which students have to work out how to tackle for themselves with minimum specific direction. Such tasks require students to construct an environment in which they can identify their learning needs and find ways of pursuing them within time constraints. Peer learning involves a group of students taking collective responsibility for identifying their own learning needs and planning how these might be addressed. This is a vital skill in learning how to learn. It also allows students to practise the kinds of interaction needed in employment. Learning to cooperate with others to reach mutual goals is a prerequisite for operating in a complex society. Peer learning prompts the acquisition of knowledge about ways of working with others in groups and one to one, and the implications of one's own learning choices on others. Seeing the different approaches that others use can broaden the base of understanding about variation in learning (Bowden and Marton, 1998).

- *Self and peer assessment.* There are seldom enough opportunities for formative assessment and getting feedback from staff in order to develop skills and concepts significantly. Peer learning settings provide opportunities for additional self and peer assessment of a formative kind. It provides opportunities for giving and receiving feedback on one's work and a context for comparing oneself to others. This mirrors the kinds of informal assessment activities that take place daily in the world of work: self-assessment and peer judgements are more common and can often have a more powerful influence in professional work than formal appraisals. Practice in identifying criteria to assess one's own learning and applying this in a variety of circumstances is a key element of sustainable assessment needed for lifelong learning (Boud, 2000).

Why does it need to be managed?

Peer learning, usually organized by students themselves, has always been a key feature of student life, but for a number of reasons these informal arrangements are beginning to break down or to be undervalued. However the experience of peer learning is known to be a significant component of a student's overall academic experience (Light, 1992) and the skills developed from working closely with peers are also considered very relevant preparation for most workplaces. This is especially the case in the project-based work environments of contemporary organizations. In order to ensure that peer learning opportunities are available to all students the processes need to be promoted and managed. This means including peer learning explicitly as part of the formal academic programme. Some responsibility for the initiation and management of these parts of courses needs to be taken by academic staff. The extent of the responsibility they take is a matter of careful judgement. If it is directed simply as another teaching task, then the benefits of students taking responsibility for their actions can be eroded and some of the potential beneficial outcomes cannot be realized. On the other hand, leaving it for students to initiate and manage may mean that it never takes place or that it only benefits a restricted group.

It is instructive to note some of the reasons why informal arrangements have been breaking down. The first reason is changes in the student profile. For many students, opportunities to meet outside class may be very limited due to work, family and other commitments. Informal meetings outside classes also favour friendship groupings and some students simply do not have the time or the social skills necessary to develop successful relationships. Such students, who may include those already disadvantaged, are therefore excluded from much of the peer learning experience. Although the need for many students to have part-time work has always had an influence on student life there is a diminishing of campus life as more students engage in more paid work. There are fewer 'full-time' students able to spend time at university talking with peers; most students have to work in some way to pay fees and living expenses. Those most in need of peer support mechanisms may therefore have least access to them.

Another reason informal peer learning may have become less common is that student populations are becoming more fragmented as students are given more choices about how they study a course. With broader subject choice, students are able to design their own progression of subjects. This means that they are less likely to be studying their course with an acknowledged class or cohort, or part of a particular home group of peers. This loss of continuity with peers can affect a student's informal learning, which traditionally has added so much to a student's university learning experience. Recent literature suggests that progress through a course with the same class can have significant and positive effects on student learning (Wesson, 1996).

Other factors that have reduced the opportunities for students to benefit from peer learning exchanges include the effects of changes in university funding. In many courses these changes have lead to the creation of larger class groups, particularly in tutorial groups. Traditionally, the purpose of tutorials was to provide students with a place to work closely with each other and to develop their ability to express, debate and discuss different points of view. These opportunities have been limited because of increases in the size of class groups.

Informal peer learning arrangements have also diminished as students have failed to recognize the important work and learning skills peer learning develops, such as interpersonal communication, team work, project management and general research and study skills. The competitive nature of many courses and the scramble for jobs after graduation may make the idea of freely sharing one's knowledge with other students seem unattractive. Some students may also refuse to believe that they can learn anything worthwhile from other students.

Thus, only by formally acknowledging peer learning within the study curriculum can appropriate recognition for the process and its outcomes be achieved (Saunders, 1992). Once students have been introduced to peer learning through planned activities, they usually realize that they have more to gain than to lose. We therefore need to provide opportunities for different types of peer learning by building relevant activities into the course of study itself. This means more than just planning a few small group discussions to fill the gaps between lectures. By managing peer learning we are formalizing what would be a highly unpredictable and selective process if left to students and their casual conversations outside the classroom, and also making the process more inclusive. Formalizing the activities also enables more deliberate review of the process and outcomes, thus making the benefits and difficulties more visible.

An important goal is to establish an environment of mutual help that continues over time and beyond the classroom. As Kail (1983) points out, if students work together only during class, then at the end of the semester, when the class has disbanded, there will be no opportunity to continue developing the group relationship. This obviously requires an institutional culture able to nurture and sustain such an environment. Peer learning will not be effective if it is introduced in isolation from other parts of the learner's life and without regard to what is happening in other parts of the course.

We need to manage the learning process in ways that draw upon the best features of traditional peer teaching and learning, without it being overly managed and prescriptive. Much of the value of these strategies for learners comes from exploration and the sense of discovery. These experiences are easily lost when prescriptive or predetermined methods are used. The key to successful peer learning, then, lies in the mutually supportive environment that learners themselves construct, and in which they feel free to express opinions, test ideas and ask for, or offer help when it is needed (Smith, 1983). Providing a structure within which this can occur is the challenge for teachers and course designers.

Does peer learning have to involve face-to-face contact?

While the original involvement of most of the contributors to this book arose from working with students in face-to-face settings, new interest has arisen more recently from those confronting the challenges of learning online. In courses where students meet each other in person, normal social interaction creates opportunities for peer learning at every turn. These opportunities have to be used by students and may need to be prompted by teachers, but they often exist without prompting. In distance learning there is no meeting of students or interaction between them unless it is especially contrived. This observation of the obvious points to why the use of peer learning facilitated by staff is a more urgent and unavoidable concern in distance courses and online settings (Salmon, 2000).

Of course, peer learning can occur, in principle, in distance courses that rely on correspondence by conventional mail, but this is difficult and ponderous when students do not meet. Peer learning has been prompted in such courses by the use of residential summer schools or weekend workshops. The use of the Internet opens new possibilities. At the simplest level, students may exchange e-mail addresses and form a discussion list. This enables all students to have ready contact with one or more of their peers as easily as sending a single message. Discussion lists formed around groups of, say, six to twelve students can maintain dialogue with each other and readily discuss issues and collaborate on tasks. Lists comprising all students run the risk of degenerating into devices for administrative use or one way communication between tutors and students as the volume of messages in an active discussion can test the patience of the most avid learners.

The limitations of e-mail communication – overloading students and teachers and the difficulty of easily tracking discussion themes – has led to the use of Web-based discussion as the medium of choice for peer learning in distance or online courses. An environment such as WebCT, Top Class or Blackboard has the facility to host as many discussion groups in as many combinations as teachers or students choose, and there are packages such as Lotus Notes that can be used without an institutional commitment to a Web-based environment. All use what is termed 'threaded discussion' to display those who have contributed on each subject. There is a record of which contributions have been read and responses can be made as easily as clicking to reply and simply typing a contribution. Students can simply discuss an issue or use a discussion forum as a means of working together on a common task. The only disadvantage this medium has over the use of e-mail is that those using the environment have to log in specially to see the discussion. This is more than balanced by the ease of navigation.

These two uses are the 'bread and butter' of peer learning among students at a distance and have become so commonplace that they are hardly worth mentioning in discussions of innovation. There are more sophisticated forms and uses of online learning, which are discussed in Stephenson (2001) and later in this book. A number of the developments in the use of computers in peer learning are taking place under the heading of computer-supported collaborative learning (CSCL). There have been bi-annual international conferences on CSCL since 1995 and a substantial literature is now available (for example, McConnell, 1999). Many of the practices described do not involve peer learning as such, but there are still good examples of this to be found there.

What led to the production of this book?

The project that eventually led to this book started five years ago. Four of us (the present editors and our late colleague, Geoff Anderson) working in what was then the School of Adult Education at the University of Technology, Sydney (UTS) identified a common interest in our own teaching. We all placed a great emphasis on students learning from each other. We were using different strategies and teaching different topics across the range from undergraduate to doctoral level, but we shared a concern that our exclusively adult students should engage in study that was personally meaningful to them and that involved them in working well with each other. We were using student-led workshops, study groups, team projects, student-to-student learning partnerships and peer feedback sessions. The four of us put together a successful proposal for a National Teaching Development Grant. This enabled us to document and analyse our existing practices, evaluate their effects on students and make them available to others. Key features of the guide produced as a result of this project have been incorporated into the present book.

Not content to limit these ideas to a Faculty of Education, we recruited collaborators to extend the exploration of peer learning practices to other disciplines and professional areas. Very interesting examples of peer learning were taking place in business, law, design, information technology and engineering at UTS and these greatly extended the repertoire of peer learning approaches that could be considered, not least into the area of online learning. The students involved included recent school leavers and in some cases much higher numbers of overseas students than was the case in the original adult education study. In order to assist other teachers in higher education to benefit from the combined experience, we considered that the best way would be to bring these approaches together in the present book.

What does the book emphasize?

The contributions to this book focus primarily on the use of peer learning in coursework programmes. There is considerable use made of peer activities in research degree studies, particularly in professional doctorates, and in clinical work and field placements, but the special demands of these contexts demand treatment in their own right. The focus here is on the normal undergraduate and postgraduate classes that most teaching staff in higher education deal with on a regular basis.

The book is structured in two parts. The first addresses the key features of peer learning: How can peer learning activities be designed and incorporated into courses (Chapter 2)? What are some common approaches used in higher education courses (Chapter 3)? How can peer learning activities be managed effectively (Chapter 4)? And what are some of the key issues involved in peer learning and assessment (Chapter 5)? These chapters are written by the editors and draw extensively on their experience in using peer learning in courses in education, mainly with adult education students.

The second part of the book broadens the disciplinary base of examples of subjects in which peer learning has been used. The authors come from the areas of design, management, law, information technology and engineering. They describe different examples of applications of peer learning in their own courses. Their case studies illustrate the different cultures of higher education disciplines and each picks up a particular theme.

In 'Team-based learning in management education' (Chapter 6) Ray Gordon and Robert Connor describe their experiences in using peer learning to pursue the important objectives of promoting student autonomy and focusing on new organizational forms within a large MBA programme. They faced the particular challenges of students from diverse backgrounds working with each other in groups.

Jenny Toynbee Wilson in 'Project management teams: a model of best practice in design' (Chapter 7) also simulates the group-based nature of work, but with first-year undergraduate students studying design. Individual project work is difficult in large classes but through peer learning in group projects she was able to more effectively reproduce the experience of working in teams while providing students with opportunities to get feedback on their design activities through peer assessment.

Jim Cooper teaches law, and in 'Peer learning in law: using a group journal' (Chapter 8) he shows how, like Ray Gordon and Robert Connor in management, he has used group journals. His emphasis is quite different to that in the management course: the focus in management was on learning about working in a group; in law it was to appreciate current legal issues. This chapter examines the issues surrounding the use of the journal, and the problems of designing, introducing and implementing a journal within the context of an introductory subject.

Information technology and computing courses frequently use project work, but Brian Lederer and Richard Raban in 'Autonomy, uncertainty and peer learning in IT project work' (Chapter 9) place particular emphasis on students learning without the intervention of tutors and on how they have used group assessment.

Chapters 10 and 11 in this section explore the use of peer learning through electronic-mediated communication. Robert McLaughlan and Denise Kirkpatrick in 'Peer learning using computer supported roleplay-simulations' (Chapter 10) describe an innovative combination of peer learning and computer mediated simulations to teach about the social, political, economic and scientific dimensions of decision making. These processes have been used with senior undergraduate and postgraduate students, bringing students from engineering to work collaboratively with political science students, and students from engineering to work with students from geology.

Mark Freeman and Jo McKenzie in 'Aligning peer assessment with peer learning for large classes: the case for an online self and peer assessment system' (Chapter 11) provide an account of working with large undergraduate classes in business. They show how self and peer-assessment can play a key role in motivating the positive outcomes of teamwork and inhibiting the possible negative aspects given the strong links between assessment, student effort and learning. They consider how self and peer ratings can also be used to encourage peer learning when used for formative feedback purposes and show how they have operationalized this through a Web-based strategy.

The third section includes the closing commentary on the key issues raised by the book. It locates peer learning as a vital element of course design in an era in which the use of teaching staff will be limited. It points to how peer learning is an integral part of a high quality learning environment and identifies some important questions that need to be addressed if peer learning is to develop further.

References

Assiter, A (ed) (1995) *Transferable Skills in Higher Education,* Kogan Page, London

Boud, D (1988) Moving towards autonomy, in *Developing Student Autonomy in Learning*, 2nd edn, ed D Boud, Kogan Page, London

Boud, D (2000) Sustainable assessment: rethinking assessment for the learning society. *Studies in Continuing Education,* **22** (2), pp 151–67

Boud, D and Walker D (1998) Promoting reflection in professional courses: the challenge of context. *Studies in Higher Education,* **23** (2), pp 191–206

Bowden, J and Marton, F (1998) *The University of Learning: Beyond quality and competence in higher education,* Kogan Page, London

Brookfield, S and Preskill, S (1999). *Discussion as a Way of Teaching,* Open University Press, Buckingham

Bruffee, K (1999) *Collaborative Learning: Higher education, interdependence and the authority of knowledge,* 2nd edn, The Johns Hopkins University Press, Baltimore

Candy, P, Crebert, G and O'Leary, J (1994) *Developing Lifelong Learners Through Undergraduate Education NBEET, Commissioned Report No 28,* Australian Government Publishing Service, Canberra

Chalmers, D and Volet, S (1997) Common misconceptions about students from South-East Asia in Australia, *Higher Education Research and Development,* **16** (1), pp 87–98

Collier, G (ed) (1983) *The Management of Peer-group Learning: Syndicate methods in higher education,* SRHE, Guildford

Falchikov, N (2001) *Learning Together: Peer tutoring in higher education,* Routledge, London

Griffiths, S, Houston, K and Lazenbatt, A (1995) *Enhancing Student Learning Through Peer Tutoring in Higher Education,* Educational Development Unit, University of Ulster, Coleraine

Jacob, E (1999) *Cooperative Learning in Context*, State University of New York Press, Albany NY

Jaques, D (2000) *Learning in Groups,* 3rd edn, Kogan Page, London

Johnson, D and Johnson, F (1997) *Joining Together: Group theory and group skills,* 6th edn, Allyn & Bacon, Boston

Kail, H (1983) Collaborative learning in context: the problem with peer tutoring, *College English,* 45 (6), pp 594–99

Light, J (1992) *Explorations with Students and Faculty about Teaching, Learning, and Student Life, The Harvard Assessment Seminars Second Report 1992,* Harvard University, Cambridge MA

Mayer, E (1992) *Putting General Education to Work: The key competency report,* Committee to Advise the Australian Education Council and the Ministers of Vocational Education, Employment and Training on Employment-related Key Competencies for Postcompulsory Education and Training, Australian Government Publishing Service, Canberra

McConnell, D (1999) *Implementing Computer Supported Cooperative Learning,* 2nd edn, Kogan Page, London

Salmon, G (2000) *E-Moderating: The key to teaching and learning online,* Kogan Page, London

Saunders D (1992) Peer tutoring in higher education, *Studies in Higher Education,* **17** (2), pp 211–18

Slavin R (1995) *Cooperative Learning,* Allyn & Bacon, Boston

Smith, D L and Hatton, N (1993) Reflection in teacher education: a study in progress, *Educational Research and Perspectives,* **20** (1), pp 13–23

Smith, R M (1983) *Learning How to Learn,* Buckingham Open University Press

Stephenson, J (ed) (2001) *Teaching and Learning Online: Pedagogies for new technologies,* Kogan Page, London

Stephenson, J and Yorke, M (eds) (1998) *Capability and Quality in Higher Education,* Kogan Page, London

Topping, K (1996) The effectiveness of peer tutoring in further and higher education: a typology and review of the literature, *Higher Education,* **32** (3), pp 321–45

Wesson, L (1996) Cohesion or collusion: impact of a cohort structure on educational leadership doctoral students, Paper presented at the Annual Meeting of the American Educational Research Association, April, New York NY

Wright, P (1995) *What Are Graduates? Clarifying the attributes of 'graduateness',* Quality Enhancement Group, The Higher Education Quality Council (HEQC), London

Part one

Basic considerations

2

Designing peer learning

Jane Sampson and Ruth Cohen

In this chapter we examine ways in which peer learning practices can be integrated into subjects or courses and designed to enable students to learn most effectively from them. The projects in which we have been engaged have highlighted the importance of formalizing peer learning within academic courses and designing it explicitly to meet desired learning outcomes. We have observed that, commonly, peer learning processes are 'add ons' to a course, and their development tends to occur 'on-the-run'. As a result the ways in which students respond to, and work with, peer learning processes do not always enable them to achieve the learning outcomes that have been intended. This leads to the learning potential of these processes being rarely realized.

Peer learning practices are usually selected because individual lecturers believe they enhance students' experience of learning, and enable them to engage in learning processes that reflect those work practices in which they will be expected to participate later, when they are in the workplace. Sometimes the initial reasons for using peer learning strategies are more pragmatic; they are seen as ways of managing the increasingly large groups of students that lecturers meet each semester.

Whatever the form peer learning takes – whether it involves students working in small study groups where they present a workshop for their class group, or students working in pairs in a learning partnership to assist each other – it is most successful when it is designed as an integral part of the overall course or subject.

It has become clear to us that the use of peer learning practices cannot just be 'added-on' to a course, or remain solely dependent on the interest and initiative of individual staff members. Rather, they need to be built into the design of the subject, or the overall course, and a number of issues need to be addressed in the implementation of the practices. Many of these considerations are a usual part of the course design process if the course is new, but if peer learning is introduced into an existing course or subject, we have found these issues are not always given sufficient attention.

The design features that we have found important include:

- considering the context into which the peer learning practice is to be introduced;
- focusing on general goals and learning outcomes;
- ensuring congruence between the peer learning strategies and assessment tasks;
- considering resource implications.

A focus on design alone is not enough. There are implementation aspects that we also believe are necessary. These involve:

- preparation of students and staff for working with the particular peer learning strategies, and their continuing roles and responsibilities;
- managing the process;
- the introduction, support and evaluation of the peer learning process.

In this chapter we describe these design features and discuss some of the issues to be considered in selecting the appropriate form of peer learning. The implementation issues will be discussed in Chapter 4.

The need to consider design issues

If we believe that peer learning practices are important teaching and learning strategies then it is necessary to ensure that the practices work successfully. For students, their engagement with any particular peer learning practice is necessarily coloured by their previous experience of working in this or similar ways. Co-operative learning practices are commonly used in schools, while students with experience of the workplace may be familiar with practices of work teams or groups. Students who have enjoyed positive and successful peer learning experiences in these contexts are likely to welcome the opportunity to work with their peers. Others may not be so inclined.

When students value peer learning practices they usually describe them as challenging, creative, exciting, and supportive. They are often surprised how much they learn about themselves, their beliefs and attitudes, as well as the subject content. Those who resist peer learning practices may express frustration about working with fractured groups and with peers who do not attempt to contribute to the learning experience. Some may perceive the practices as having little, if any, obvious purpose or guidelines. Their reactions are a function of both their prior negative experiences and the current activities in which they are involved.

To involve these students effectively and ensure that the peer learning practices work well, the design and implementation issues we have named need to be addressed. Without these our experience has been that students become confused, uncertain about how to proceed, and feel unsupported and sceptical about the value of what they are doing. They focus on the inadequacies of the process rather than on what they are using it for. These counterproductive reactions can be addressed relatively easily. There may still be issues to be resolved for particular students, but these can be more readily addressed when we are confident that most students are operating effectively.

When the peer learning activity is designed so that the guidelines are clear, the purpose relates to students' needs, the practice is linked appropriately to the assessment process and the learning outcomes, and students are prepared for the experience, students can benefit from the positive features of peer learning.

Design features

The following design features are not independent. As in any course design process, each stage or element affects the others. However in describing them it is useful to identify each separately.

Considering context

The first feature is consideration of the context into which the peer learning practice is to be introduced. The context includes not just the physical and organizational aspects of the course but the assumptions and expectations that impinge on students. This encompasses the educational beliefs and values underpinning the design of the subject or course – is it, for example, intentionally cooperative or competitive? It also takes into account the focus of the educational philosophies and beliefs about learning, both espoused and practised in the faculty or course, for which the peer learning activity is proposed. For example, is the course fully learner-centred or is it oriented primarily around the needs of the discipline or profession?

In considering context it is also necessary to recognize the expectations, experience and beliefs about learning that students and staff bring to the faculty and the course, and to acknowledge how it is intended the students should be prepared for their future workplaces. This in turn includes noticing and working with cultural and gender differences and accommodating these in the new approach (Boud and Walker, 1998).

Teaching and learning values

Underlying values about teaching and learning might be reflected in the structural features of a course that is 'content' driven by the way time is allocated to theory and practice within the course. Similarly, in a 'content' driven course, it is likely that the subject matter, the knowledge and skills to be learned, and the process, the way in which they will be learned, are determined and controlled by the teacher with little or no negotiation with the students. In such a learning climate staff may find peer learning strategies more difficult to accept as the strategies tend to give considerable freedom to students to make various decisions about their learning. This may include students making decisions about how they proceed and even what they might learn within a particular framework. The teacher might guide but not direct specific content outcomes. Within any one peer learning structure some students may be learning more from the experience of the process and others might be learning more from the topic they are exploring. The students are directing much of their learning.

In Chapter 10, McLaughlan and Kirkpatrick describe a particular context where the students came from different academic cultures, bringing quite different academic knowledge and academic cultural understanding from their different disciplines. Within this context a key theme was the exchange of knowledge and the development of some of the more generic interpersonal and group skills. Individual students were likely to focus on different learning outcomes although the development of some of the more generic communication and interpersonal skills was also very important to them.

Peer learning strategies can be introduced most profitably when the values of the programme support them. A strong degree of learner-centredness is required. This would include acceptance that different students will learn different things, that learning outcomes related to wider learning skills are as important as particular subject-matter understandings and that students should be encouraged to make their own decisions about their learning.

Learning as an individual activity

Another contextual issue is presented when the dominant philosophy of learning in a faculty or course regards learning as a competitive and individual activity. This tends to place the emphasis on students being taught and assessed rather than on their development of learning skills. A programme with this perspective would probably require high levels of content to be 'transmitted' to the students in the limited time available and students would be expected to assimilate this on an individual basis rather than collaborating or cooperating with others. In some contexts assessment may still be regarded as a competitive process notwithstanding an institutional shift to criterion-based assessment. Such contexts would not support general peer collaboration and may even have processes in use that could limit the benefits of such activities. Such a climate is likely to make the introduction of peer learning strategies quite difficult and at best the range of peer learning approaches fruitfully adopted is likely to be limited.

Ironically, extremely competitive and selective courses can foster informal peer learning among students, for the very reason that informal approaches are typically exclusionary – an in-group of students cooperates in order to beat others. In such a context, formal approaches intended to be inclusive may meet resistance from those who feel that their dominant role is likely to be challenged.

Students' experiences of learning

Students who have successfully 'learnt to learn' as individuals can find that the process of learning with others creates some discomfort, and some students used to more teacher-centred learning approaches can find it difficult to identify what they are learning from the experience. In addition some students suggest that they do not have the skills or the desire to deal with issues such as managing the group process, non-attendance, 'freeloading', conflict, and peers who do not like each other.

Similar resistance may be displayed by students who believe that in formal courses they are there to learn from the lecturer. These students may find it difficult to accept that their peers have anything to teach them, or indeed that they have anything of value to teach their peers. A common concern is that what they learn from peers will be flawed in some way, that it might be a situation where the ignorant lead the unknowing. It is obviously important in such a climate to address these concerns and establish how peer-learning strategies are beneficial.

The students themselves may generate a competitive learning climate, because of the way they have learned to learn, in which case the use of peer learning strategies may be intended to bring about a change in their attitudes to learning. In such a climate the peer learning strategy selected and the way it is introduced would need to be planned carefully to overcome any resistance.

When a course is already overloaded with content or assessment activities, additional activities requiring students to engage in peer learning will be given low priority. Students may respond cynically to the introduction of peer learning when it is an addition to an already overloaded curriculum. Just because informal peer learning groups emerge when students are stretched does not mean that staff can formalize these groups in the same circumstances without resistance. Students will, not unreasonably, regard the use of organized peer learning in this situation as a way of avoiding the problem of designing and staffing an effective course.

Peer learning is effective when there is a willingness to focus on learning as a social as well as an individual activity, a desire for the development of skills in cooperating and working with each other and a valuing of the importance of students challenging each other. Time devoted to peer learning must be seen not as a diminution of time devoted to the content of the course, but as a way of equipping students to engage with it more effectively. This may mean that in the short term, less is 'covered', but the investment of time made in developing the learning skills of students has a pay-off later in the extended repertoire of students' learning skills.

Taking account of 'difference'

Working with peers highlights the importance of understanding and working with the idea of difference. The word 'difference' here means more than just differences occurring between individuals. Studies of learning in social settings have shown that the ways in which others treat different groups of learners in the same context – both staff and students – are profoundly influenced by the broader social context. Students' experiences of comfort, safety and their opportunities to learn within a group are often addressed through a group set of expectations of the subject, the task and the others with whom they work. Male and female students, for example, tend to be treated differently by both male and female staff, solely by virtue of their gender. Similarly, students and staff from particular ethnic groups are treated differently by both students and staff from other ethnic groups. Other differences may relate to age, disability, nationality, sexual orientation and other features that have no relationship at all to what is being learned. The ways in which people relate to and respond to others varies greatly. These responses can inhibit or enhance any learning activity.

A collaborative learning approach may suit many learners. It has been much discussed that women, for example, find relationships in learning, particularly with peers, important to their learning experience (Schneider, 1969; Belenky et al., 1986; Hayes, 1989). As Maher and Tetreault observed: 'The traditional discourse silenced her, not only because of the subject matter, but also because of her preference for "connected" relational learning often observed in women students' (Maher and Tetreault, 1994: 100).

The challenge of 'difference' in peer learning is twofold. Firstly, it prompts us to think about how to use differences between participants productively pertinent to the task in hand. Secondly, it highlights the need to avoid the kinds of stereotyping, oppressive and offensive behaviour that get in the way of everyone's learning – including that of the oppressors. If these challenges are not met, the potential of peer learning will not be realized and the risk that oppressive practices will be reinforced will be ever present. Of course, the risks are present even when staff conduct activities, but teachers have a professional obligation to ensure that they actively promote students productively learning from one another and to confront inappropriate behaviour. Students need to be equipped to do the same in peer learning settings. Ray Gordon and Robert Connor in Chapter 6 discuss some of these issues of difference that business students experienced in working in culturally diverse groups in a subject in their MBA.

This issue is not easy to address and considerable thought needs to be given to suitable approaches. Two general approaches appear to be used commonly. The first of these is to construct peer learning activities so that they emphasize student cooperation, working together, collaborative activities, mutuality and shared responsibility. In this approach, processes that celebrate differences and avoid negative manifestations of difference are built into the briefing, guidelines and structure of activities. Difference is seen as implicit, without raising the issue, directly. This approach is appropriate in many circumstances and it means that interventions by staff are limited to when problems arise. Nevertheless staff do need to be prepared to deal with the inevitable manifestation of issues when they appear to be seriously getting in the way of learning.

The second approach draws explicit attention to matters of 'difference' from the very start. In this approach staff signal the importance of building on difference and confronting oppressive behaviour. They attempt to set a context in which difference is explicit by providing frameworks for thinking about it and for introducing ways of working productively with it. Depending on the nature of the student group and its purpose, this might include theoretical input about power and oppression, examples of strategies that can be used and opportunities to practise forms of intervention. Pettman (1991) provides a good illustration of such an approach. She suggests that anyone conducting a learning activity should always start with the assumption of difference not sameness.

It is tempting for staff committed to fighting oppression to adopt the second approach but there is a risk in doing so when institutional policies and culture are not sufficiently oriented towards celebrating difference. The risk is one of provoking the very problems one is wishing to avoid and setting a group on a course where their agenda becomes one of working on oppression rather than dealing with the learning tasks they were established for in the first place. This is not to argue that there should not be opportunities within any course for this to occur, because it can be a valuable way of having students confront and understand the issues of oppression. However it is usually most effective when students are also studying these issues and the subject of oppression is the focus of their learning. Without this background, there is the danger that merely raising these issues may engender fear and anxiety and act to silence members of non-dominant groups. Accordingly, if developing awareness about issues of difference, power and oppression is actually one of the learning outcomes, then the second approach is appropriate. If not, then the first is probably preferable. Certainly staff working with students using either approach need to be comfortable addressing these issues. Unfortunately, even when you know there is an issue and you try to do something about it, things can go wrong.

We are not suggesting that peer learning structures can only survive in an ideal context with the 'correct' educational philosophy and practices. Where there are obvious differences in the values reflected in peer learning strategies and in course philosophy, the introduction of peer learning just needs to be carried out carefully. It is important to ensure that staff and students have time to adjust to the different learning opportunities and to their own changed roles within the processes, whilst being mindful of possible disruptions from those whose positions are threatened.

General goals and learning outcomes

The second design feature focuses on the general goals and the learning objectives or outcomes of the subject or course. It involves the fitting or matching of the peer learning strategy to the course's overall goals and the more specific desired learning outcomes or learning objectives, and necessarily, to the group of students and their future learning.

When selecting any teaching and learning strategy it is obviously important to ensure that the strategy will enable the students to achieve what is intended and that students are informed about what is expected of them. This is no less the case with peer learning, but is more likely to be overlooked if peer learning is seen only as something which is 'generally helpful' to students. There needs to be clarification about just what knowledge should be acquired, what skills need to be developed, whether they are skills directly related to the topic area or more generic learning skills, and what affective change is desired.

The very nature of peer learning processes, involving students fully in an experience, means that many things might be learned from it. When students first enter a course it might be important that their engagement in reciprocal peer learning activities is used to increase their interpersonal and group communication skills, and to increase their contact with their peers while also beginning to explore the content area of the subject. Ideally the experience will also prepare them to manage more complex peer learning experiences at a later stage of the course. At another stage in the course the design of the learning experience may relate more directly to preparing students for a specific professional environment.

Frequently the peer learning experience is intended to achieve a number of objectives, both course based and professionally focused. In Chapter 7, Jenny Wilson writes about the way she structures a peer learning strategy for first-year design students to develop in students certain skills that are linked directly to the professional area in which they will ultimately work. The practice enables them to learn to critique their work and the work of their peers, a practice that they will experience throughout the course and within the design industry when they enter it.

Yet another consideration is whether the learning outcomes associated with the peer learning are given sufficient importance within the course to justify spending time on them. It is necessary to identify which outcomes are the most important in any given context and to design activities that help students achieve them.

Similarly in Chapter 9 Brian Lederer and Richard Raban write about their use of project-based peer learning in the final year of a computing degree. This peer learning activity is designed to model the work groups students are expected to work in once they enter the computer industry. The learning outcomes relate to the development of their professional technical abilities as well as their abilities to perform in work teams.

In teacher education courses we might structure the peer learning strategy to encourage the students to reflect on their learning experiences with a view to considering how they might use similar strategies with their learners when they become practising teachers.

Other considerations in designing the peer learning practices might focus on the overall process issues within the course itself such as creating a positive learning climate. A peer learning activity might be introduced in the first semester in order to help students mix with a greater number of students from the very beginning of their course. Jim Cooper, in Chapter 8, describes this as a significant objective in his use of a peer learning strategy with first year students. Gradually peer learning strategies might be introduced that require students to have greater levels of confidence about their skills and knowledge.

In using particular peer learning strategies the achievement of some objectives is of higher priority than others. Some objectives will be fore-grounded by assessment tasks, whereas other objectives will be achieved in order to complete the necessary assessment requirements but they may remain in the background. Some learning outcomes will be assessed and others may remain important to the overall development of the learner, and not be formally assessed.

It is necessary to be very clear about the desired specific and general outcomes. Many of the learning outcomes pursued by peer learning activities tend to be generic rather than subject-specific, so they can easily be lost or the assumption made that they will be developed elsewhere. Generic learning outcomes often resulting from peer learning experiences include interpersonal communication skills, negotiation skills, teamwork and presentation skills. In a particular peer learning experience only one of these, like presentation skills, might be assessed, yet students may have learned and developed relevant skills in the other areas that are not directly assessed.

As learning is increasingly viewed from a lifelong perspective, further consideration in regard to learning outcomes extends to the transfer of the learning, how this learning might be used in other contexts and how it might contribute to further learning. Learning how to learn with and from peers is in itself a skill that contributes to lifelong learning and it is one on which students will depend extensively when they begin their practice in their chosen professions.

Congruence between learning strategies and assessment tasks

Assessment can challenge the principles of peer learning by creating an inappropriately competitive environment. Equally the absence of assessment can devalue the process by failing to provide acknowledgement of the learning that the peer process encourages. When planning to implement peer learning practices, the need to consider the congruence of those practices and the intended assessment tasks is linked directly to consideration of the learning outcomes.

If an excessively competitive climate already exists within a class, establishing any form of cooperative work is likely to be enormously difficult. When students must compete with each other for rationed places in further study, for example, there will be a limit to what can be achieved through formalized peer learning, as distrust and fear may undermine the learning outcomes. Peer learning is accepted more readily in courses where assessment is primarily criterion referenced or competency based rather than norm referenced. The relationship between assessment and peer learning is a complex one discussed in more detail in Chapter 5.

If the peer learning practice does not obviously relate to the assessment processes students may condemn it as a waste of time. Even when it is linked, some students may perceive their assessment marks are jeopardized by their reluctant peers and the time-consuming nature of the process.

The peer learning strategy used with design students, described in Chapter 7, is linked to the assessment task but it is not a group assessment task. The peer learning strategy is primarily intended to help students provide support for each other while they are engaged in individually assessed tasks. The nature of that support is to ensure that students are working on their assessment tasks, and for their peers to give them constructive feedback on their progress. Being able to give and receive constructive feedback is an important ability in most fields but it is critical in the professional practice of design. Students help each other develop these skills while also assisting each other to improve the quality of the work they are presenting for assessment. The peer learning strategy is producing outcomes that are very beneficial to the individual members because the process assists them in completing their assessment tasks.

If the assessment task involves a group assessment it is usually more effective if the selected assessment task requires the combined efforts of the peers. For instance, the final assessment task used in the peer learning practice in the computing course described in Chapter 9 requires the combined skill of a group of people; it is too large for any one student. The student experience of working in this way is more obviously worthwhile.

It is also important that guidelines for assessment are clear and equitable. In systems where grades or marks are allocated to individuals based on a group product, criteria for their distribution should be transparent; otherwise the assessment can have a divisive effect. It can work against the purpose of peer learning and undermine the development of learning outcomes such as the development of teamwork skills. A common concern is that only some of the students do the work that is rewarded. Yet others may have been responsible for maintaining the relationships in the peer group that enabled the group to function and complete the assessment tasks successfully. In Chapter 11, Mark Freeman and Jo McKenzie describe an approach to working with peer and self-assessment in a finance subject. This approach is proving successful in addressing many of these issues.

Assessment tasks need to be designed to respond to this challenge. This typically involves working through the consequences of existing assessment tasks and modifying them accordingly. It is rare to get such tasks well adjusted at the first attempt, so a progressive refinement of assessment tasks is to be expected.

Peer learning strategies are personally and intellectually demanding so it is important for students to see that the energy and effort they contribute to making these processes work is valued. There also needs to be an agreed approach determined early in the activity identifying all the learning outcomes and how they will be valued. Similarly it needs to be clear how students who do not contribute to the task or group process will fare.

Considering resource implications

Peer learning does not place significant demands on resources. In most circumstances it can be implemented within existing budgets and staffing levels. One of its attractions is that it can be conducted through relatively small variations in current staff activity. However, although the ongoing cost is not measurable there are initial modest establishment costs, principally because staff and students need to become familiar with these different approaches to teaching.

Part of the resource implication is a 'cost' in the normal use of time, particularly in the case of preparing students. Another resource implication is the expense of the materials and resources that students and staff are given to assist them in understanding the processes they are to use.

Staff development is an integral part of the change process. For some staff these changes will be a matter of degree only; for others this approach will be a major change from lecturer-directed and controlled learning to student-negotiated and managed learning. Working with student-led groups, negotiating learning and rethinking what constitutes effective learning and valid assessment procedures are issues requiring careful introduction.

Development activities for staff who work together on a course designed to help them consider the new strategies may take time initially but it is well spent as it avoids a lot of unproductive troubleshooting at a later stage. A careful introduction enables colleagues to develop ideas about how best to use these strategies in their present programmes, make the learning processes and the assessment methods congruent, and develop ways to evaluate the qualitative and quantitative outcomes of these new or modified strategies. It is also important to provide staff with materials that clearly explain the rationale for using peer learning strategies in a specific context and that conceptualizes the educational approach in a framework of university teaching and learning.

Materials provided for students, on the other hand, need to be highly specific to their course of study. Students require detailed materials explaining the rationale for the different ways of learning and assessment, and suggestions that will help them to engage effectively in peer learning. These suggestions may differ depending on the peer learning strategies being used, the timescales involved and the nature of the subject. Given that teamwork is becoming such an important part of the culture of work, the student resource package might also include effective strategies for working in groups, managing learning tasks and ways to minimize and deal with group conflict. Students may also appreciate information on how to monitor and evaluate their own progress.

As peer learning becomes a widespread practice, additional resource issues arise. Students may need locations to meet and access to equipment such as photocopiers and computer networks. There is also the potential for peer learning activities to increase the study time required, especially if staff are not aware of the amount of learning that is taking place in the new strategy. An audit of demands on students can be helpful, if only to show them that the new activities have been introduced in full awareness of the consequences.

Peer learning has been found to be especially valuable to part-time students because they have an opportunity to meet and work with their fellow students, but it is important to portray clearly the total demands of a course. For example, a timetable listing only periods of staff-student contact can be very misleading. It is sometimes useful to formally schedule peer learning periods and list them on timetables to acknowledge them as part of normal student workload. If possible, it is also useful to schedule that peer learning time bordered by other formal learning sessions, so that students are already present in the building and not just arriving or having to leave early.

Having decided to use peer learning approaches and having considered the design issues, the next step is to determine which peer learning strategy will be most appropriate and how it might need to be adapted for your context, your staff, your students and their learning needs. Deciding on an appropriate peer learning strategy requires purposeful selection and careful adaptation. This is needed to suit the context in which it will be used and to achieve the learning outcomes desired while also remaining congruent with the assessment requirements. We discuss some of the issues to be considered and some basic frameworks that might be used, in the following chapter.

References

Belenky, M, Clinchy, B, Goldberger, N and Tarule, J (1986) *Women's Ways of Knowing: The development of self, voice and mind*, Basic Books, New York

Boud, D and Walker, D (1998) Promoting reflection in professional courses: the challenge of context, *Studies in Higher Education*, **23** (2), pp 191–206

Hayes, E (1989) Insights from women's experiences for teaching and learning, in *Effective Teaching Styles* (ed) E Hayes, pp 55–65, Jossey-Bass, San Francisco

Maher, F and Tetreault, M (1994) *The Feminist Classroom*, Basic Books, New York

Pettman, J (1991) Towards a (personal) politics of location, *Studies in Continuing Education*, **13** (2), pp 153–66

Schneider, H (1969) The peer learning approach to adult learning, *Equity and Excellence*, **4** (3), pp 73–77

3

Strategies for peer learning: some examples

Jane Sampson and Ruth Cohen

There are as many ways of using peer learning in courses as there are different courses. As we have seen in the previous chapter it is necessary to tailor strategies to fit the particular characteristics of the course, its outcomes and the setting in which it takes place. However, it can also be useful to have a range of possible peer learning activities in mind to help prompt thinking about what might be available to adapt to one's own context.

In this chapter we discuss how to choose a particular strategy and consider what different strategies might be good for. We describe four strategies that we have used in different ways in our own courses and illustrate their effects through the use of students' responses to them.

Selecting strategies

While the most common situation is normally that of fitting peer learning into an existing course, we sometimes have the opportunity of offering a new course and can therefore include peer learning as an integral part of the design.

Whatever the situation, there are a variety of ways in which peer learning might be used. Some of these are:

- as one of a range of alternative teaching methods – for example as a substitute for some kinds of tutorial;
- as part of a constellation of learning strategies – for example to ensure that *all* students experience informal peer learning;

- as a strategy to remedy specific problems – for example to give students more practice in verbal presentation;
- as the central organizing feature of learning – for example as an integral feature of planning in a student-negotiated curriculum;
- as part of a holistic conception of teaching and learning – for example through explicitly acknowledging the role of peers in the total repertoire of teaching and learning experiences.

Once we determine the place of peer learning in a course there are other considerations that might influence selection of a particular peer learning strategy. Some of these have already been mentioned when discussing general design issues. They include:

- the particular learning outcomes being sought;
- students' prior experience of group work and collaborative activities;
- staff prior experience of using peer learning;
- overall workload pressures on students;
- assessment and evaluation expectations;
- practical issues such as constraints on time and place of learning.

Other considerations are present in any interpersonal or group situation and relate to specific aspects of learners' backgrounds and their learning experiences. The selection of a peer learning strategy needs to take into account the students' abilities to work with:

- differences in knowledge and experience bases;
- the potential for differences in power;
- culture-specific or gendered activities;
- the potential for oppressive behaviour by dominant group members;
- tensions between the task and the process;
- cultural norms, values and expectations in any given setting;
- group dynamics, for example the stages of the group's development.

The decision to select some strategies might be made with the intention of developing these abilities whereas others might be made with the understanding that the students will be able to manage these differences effectively so that particular learning can be achieved without having to address broader issues.

Some alternatives

There are of course many possible strategies that can be considered or adapted for particular purposes or contexts. Not every peer learning strategy is equally suitable. Some work well in small classes, some require prior expertise in group work and others are designed to address very specific learning outcomes.

Key features of all strategies are that they enable peers to work together and learn from and with each other; learn from each other's knowledge and experiences; learn through listening to each other's opinions and expressed values and beliefs; and as giving and receiving feedback from each other.

Some common activities that represent peer learning approaches include:

- *Seminar presentations* in small groups or pairs after completing a shared project or assignment.
- *Work-in-progress reports* by individuals or groups working together on a project or assignment, followed by question and discussion sessions.
- *Debriefing sessions* (in pairs, small groups or larger plenary sessions) following a field placement, industrial visit or work experience programme.
- *Peer assessments* where assignments are first marked by fellow students and then the mark or comments are discussed. The justification of marks awarded is a valuable learning experience for both parties.

As we have already discussed, the most important feature of using peer learning practices, as is the case with most approaches to teaching and learning, is that they are designed to suit the particular context, the particular learning purposes and the particular kind of learners who will be involved.

Elements of peer learning activities

There are a number of different elements used in various ways in peer learning activities. These include introductory activities, ways of working in groups, communication skills such as listening, presenting and explaining, dealing with conflict, problem solving, planning and negotiation, facilitation, reflection and journal keeping. These are documented in detail in a number of sources. While useful information can be found in these sources both for staff organizing peer learning and for the students engaged in it, usually it is necessary to translate the ideas about conventional teaching and learning contexts into the peer learning setting.

Table 3.1 Description of important topics in peer learning, and some sources for further information

Topic	Description	Sources
Introductory activities	Getting started in new groups; icebreakers	Eitington, 1996; Jones, 1991; Newstrom and Scannell, 1980, 1983, 1994, 1998; Scannell and Newstrom, 1991
Working in groups	Group functions, processes and techniques; group development	Jaques, 2000; Johnson and Johnson, 1997
Listening skills	Listening to others as a key feature of working cooperatively in a group	Knights, 1985; Brownell, 1986
Planning and negotiation	Goal setting, learning agreements and contracts	Anderson, Boud and Sampson, 1996; Knowles, 1975; Gillespie, Guthrie, Kelly and Sampson, 1992
Facilitation	Leading and inter- vening in groups	Brookfield, 1986; Galbraith, 1990; Heron, 1989, 1993, 1999; Boud and Miller, 1996
Presentation and explaining skills	Ways of conveying information and ideas that will be understood	Brown, 1978; Brown and Hatton, 1982; Brookfield, 1990; Habeshaw, et. al. 1987; Smith and Delahaye, 1998; Eitington, 1996
Problem solving	Processes for identifying, clarifying and generating solutions to problems	Woods, 1994
Dealing with conflict, group problems, sexism and racism	Addressing interpersonal and intra-group difficulties effectively	Tiberius, 1999; Jaques, 2000; Crum, 1987; Cornelius and Faire, 1989; Hayes and Colin, 1994;

		Chambers and Pettman, 1986
Reflection and journal keeping	Incorporating processes which encourage the processing of learning	Boud, Keogh and Walker, 1985; Holly, 1989; Rainer, 1980; Fulwiler, 1987; Reinertsen and Wells, 1993
Giving and receiving feedback	Providing comments to others in ways which contribute to their learning	Boud, 1995; Boud, Cohen and Walker, 1993
Self and peer assessment	The use of assessment processes consistent with the goals of peer learning	Boud, 1995; Falchikov, 1995, 2001

Table 2.1 summarizes these elements and suggests some sources for further information.

Using group projects is a common practice. These usually involve a group of students completing a set task that counts toward assessment. Students refine their conceptual understanding, acquire relevant communication skills and practical experience of group dynamics and time management skills. Apart from the content learned, the processes of negotiating and allocating appropriate roles, staging the tasks and monitoring progress for the project duration to meet deadlines are useful professional skills.

Key features of group projects are:

- groups assigned or self-selected;
- they are usually limited to three to seven persons;
- they aim to produce a substantial piece of work;
- assessment criteria allocated by staff; negotiation may be possible;
- assessment results by staff or peers may be assigned individually or as a group mark;
- organizing roles, workloads, and time management skills.

Later chapters of this book discuss a range of specific peer learning practices used in a number of different faculties. They are described within the particular contexts for which they were designed. However they present possible models of strategies that can be adapted for other contexts and purposes. Chapters

10 and 11 reflect the general principles of group projects described above with features particular to their faculty and work contexts.

Four useful strategies

The strategies most commonly used within our own courses are:

- *Learning partnerships*: one-to-one learning relationships involving occasional meetings in which students support each other's learning.
- *Study groups*: either a formal (staff-facilitated) or informal (student-directed) strategy for learning about working in small groups, exchanging learning and providing peer support during the course.
- *Student-led workshops:* students work together to plan and conduct a workshop for their colleagues, thus learning about working as a team member while researching and preparing the workshop content, and marketing, conducting and evaluating the workshop.
- *Learning exchanges*: formal student presentations to a small group of peers so students learn about a topic directly from their peers, whilst also learning from the experience of delivering their own presentations and observing their peers' presentation approaches, and learning from giving and receiving critical feedback.

Our students have reported that they have found the strategies effective, but they also provide basic frameworks that have potential to be adapted for use in a broad range of higher education contexts. They are described in more detail below.

Learning partnerships

A learning partnership is a relationship in which a student purposefully plans, learns and reflects with a peer of his or her own choice (Robinson et al., 1985). Partners generally engage with academic issues at a deeper level than if working alone. The support generated through this peer relationship is an important factor for academic development. Learning partnerships are characterized by openness and active discussion of ideas and processes and provide relevant experience for continuing professional development.

The key features of learning partnerships are:

- partners are self-chosen;
- there is regular contact at mutually convenient times;

- learning agendas are negotiated;
- set readings are discussed, partners engage with concepts and try out ideas;
- class sessions are reviewed;
- partners give reciprocal feedback to each other on assignment writing;
- content is related to their own experiences;
- different perspectives and interpretations are made explicit;
- partners provide mutual support to each other.

Some student comments about learning partnerships were:

> I found it strange working this way at first, you have to organize your time a bit differently and you have to think about someone else's needs.

> A word of advice – spend some time at the beginning getting to know each other and working out what you want from the partnership.

> I did not want to work this way but having done it I would recommend it now. My learning partner helped me edit my writing, and seeing how someone else approached the issues helped me think differently about what I did.

> I liked having someone I could ring to talk about any problems I had getting started or in understanding the textbook.

> It has been fantastic, we began working in a learning partnership in first semester of our course because it was a subject requirement, but we have stayed helping each other through first and second year.

Study groups

Study groups are usually semi–autonomous student groups established to explore course-related matters collaboratively or they may be fully autonomous groups responsible for their own learning agendas with no formal group assessment.

Membership of study groups may be through self-selection. However it is usually more successful if it is organized in a more neutral way that promotes diversity. If all students are involved in determining the criteria for group membership the process is generally accepted as more equitable.

The staff member's role is essentially to introduce the students to the process, and suggest guidelines on how they might function. Staff may provide resources for the group and be available when appropriate to facilitate negotiations within the group if its members are unable to work together effectively. The staff member usually maintains some regular contact with the groups to monitor their progress. Study groups provide a personal support network in which students discuss course-related content, receive feedback on their ideas and actions and make contributions to each other's learning.

Study groups may be required to provide a regular written report on the group's progress to the subject or course co-ordinator and where appropriate present information to other class members about specific learning experiences the group may have had.

Academic outcomes include using the language of the subject effectively, clarifying concepts and issues in greater depth, negotiating issues requiring group decisions, and developing research and learning strategies. Commonly mentioned student learning outcomes include a more realistic understanding of group dynamics, effective meeting skills and professional and cultural knowledge.

Key features of study groups include the following:

- groups comprise five to seven students;
- regular meetings are timetabled outside class sessions but when all students are available to attend;
- they provide access to a range of skills and experiences;
- students experience how groups operate;
- groups work more-or-less independently on set or negotiated tasks;
- products of the study groups are generally assessed by the groups themselves, staff and/or by the larger class group.

Students' comment about study groups include the following:

Expect to be challenged more than you expected!

Establish the ground rules at the beginning. Be flexible.

Take a risk, try all the ideas you can. . . and learn from the experience.

Be aware of differences and make the most of them.

An excellent opportunity to try new ways in what feels like a safe environment.

Keep a learning journal – it helps.

If you allow time to talk about where you are all coming from it might make different learning styles and needs more easy to comprehend and understand.

Talk about group process – meet regularly – try some 'fuzzy things' to sort out the group dynamics. Be brave and ask for what you want.

Get to know each other – strengths, weaknesses, issues. . .

Have a huge argument at the beginning. . . please!

Student-led workshops

In small groups, students research, design, market, conduct and evaluate a workshop for their peers in the larger class. The group determines or negotiates what the workshop will be about, ensuring that it has a relevance for other students, the course and subject.

The learning outcomes may be many and varied. There is learning within the workshop group; learning about planning, marketing, presenting and evaluating a workshop, learning about the workshop content, learning about group processes, group decision making, delegation, and learning about teaching and learning strategies and team teaching or co-facilitating. It is generally useful to encourage each member of the workshop group to decide early in the process on what he or she wants to learn from the overall experience of working in the workshop group. Without some focus students can find themselves overwhelmed with the experience and unsure of what they are learning.

For the larger class there is also learning on a number of levels. There is learning related to the content of the workshop, and learning about how others have conducted the workshop.

The staff member has a monitoring role to ensure that the design of the workshop is both appropriate for members of the larger class group and that the workshop group is planning and presenting something that will be a worthwhile learning experience for members of their own group. It is useful to include a regular method of reporting so that the staff member has some knowledge of what is being planned.

Sometimes costs are incurred by the group, which they are expected to cover, but the staff member may need to keep a wary eye on the workshop management and financial arrangements to ensure that costs are kept to a minimum.

Academic outcomes include greater understanding of subject matter through working with subject content to teach it to others, developing research and learning strategies, using the language of the subject effectively and negotiating issues which require group decisions. Commonly mentioned student learning outcomes include a more realistic understanding of group dynamics, effective planning, marketing, team teaching, and presentation skills as well as increased professional and cultural knowledge.

Key features of a student-led workshop include:

- the planning and presentation group size is between three and eight members;
- a reporting system is used to keep staff briefed about developments;
- time is allocated for the workshop to be presented to the wider student group;
- students with different levels of experience or ability are accommodated as there are so many learning opportunities within the process.

Students' comments about student-led workshops included the following:

Get good channels of communication going.

Have focus, have fun!

Get that 'idea' which the group responds to for a workshop early on.

Do what people are interested in and something everyone will enjoy.

Deal with issues as they come up. Don't suppress!

Have achievable goals. Enjoy the learning.

Be flexible in delivering the workshop. Great opportunity to learn from others within the group.

Learning exchanges

Learning exchanges provide a forum in which students can learn from their peers whilst also helping their peers learn. It involves practising presentation or facilitation skills through students teaching a small group of their peers about a particular topic or how to perform a specific skill. It may also involve creating an activity that challenges their peers' thinking and beliefs about an issue.

A common expectation among the different disciplines is that a professional practitioner is able to present information to his or her colleagues. Practitioners need to be able to present information, or teach others about aspects of their work or about their organization generally. The learning exchange is a way that students can develop these skills while learning from the presentation content and the processes used by their peers.

A learning exchange involves students working in groups of five to eight people and where possible it is best held over one day as a workshop. That way all students are involved in the same process at the one time. The small groups each need a room of their own to avoid distractions.

Students are expected to prepare their presentation and plan how they intend presenting it. Within the learning exchange itself they might be allocated 20 or 30 minutes to give their presentation. The presenter allows for questions about the topic within this time span. A further 15 or 20 minutes is then scheduled for each presenter immediately following his or her presentation for discussion about the way in which the topic was presented and the impact of the presentation. Within the learning exchange students manage the equal distribution of time and give feedback to each other about the presentations.

The role of staff is to prepare students for the learning exchange. This includes briefing on the nature of the experience, equipping students with presentation guidelines and processes for giving feedback to presenters. Staff may also need to organize the accommodation and resources required, and monitor progress of the day. The staff member usually needs to facilitate the debriefing and group reflection on the learning that follows the learning exchange.

The learning outcomes include students learning from their own presentations and the presentations of others. They learn about the specific subject matter, presentation, self-management and develop skills in giving and receiving feedback. Key features include:

- preparation of students for the experience;
- students commit time to preparing their presentations;
- students work in groups of five to eight;
- there is equal time for each presentation and for group discussion and feedback to the presenter;
- timing guidelines are provided;

- the group schedules the order of presentations;
- feedback guidelines are provided;
- staff facilitate group reflection and debriefing of the overall activity.

Students' comments about learning exchanges included the following:

Approach with an open mind. Listen, hear and enjoy. Everything in the learning exchange helps you to grow.

Before the learning exchange – worry and plan. . . *During* the session – practical and still worry. . . After – great experience and self-discovery!

Good opportunity to see changes in self and others.

Presentations are good and extra knowledge. Enjoy it.

You are being asked to *do* something rather than just *talk* about it!

The more you participate, the more you will learn.

Good opportunity to share with fellow students – different styles.

Enlightening. See yourself as others see you. Confidence boosting.

Excellent opportunity to practise and learn from your peers.

The best experience! Prepare and reap the benefits.

It is a real learning process – a really inspiring and enlightening experience.

Relating strategies to learning outcomes

Each of the four strategies has a different emphasis. Some are more effective at pursuing particular learning outcomes than others. Table 3.2 summarizes the extent to which the four peer learning strategies contribute to the achievement of different identified learning outcomes. As this table indicates,

Table 3.2 Extent to which reciprocal peer learning strategies contribute to learning outcomes

Learning outcomes	Peer learning strategy			
	Learning partnerships	Study groups	Student-led workshops	Learning exchanges
Articulating understanding				
Planning				
Rehearsing				
Presenting				
Giving feedback				
Reflection				
Negotiating learning				
Working in groups				
Peer support				
Peer assessment				

Key: Indicates how well each peer learning strategy contributes to the learning outcome

Little contribution	Part contribution, depending on form of implementation	Major contribution

the level of contribution to particular learning outcomes is usually dependent on the way in which the peer learning approach is implemented.

The four strategies we have chosen to describe are not intended as templates for reciprocal peer learning activities. They are certainly not intended as prescriptions to be followed but are merely what we have found to be effective practices in the settings we have examined. While this chapter does not explore a great many strategies in detail, the discussion of the strategies that were studied will hopefully provide general guidance.

As with any approach to teaching and learning the most important feature of peer learning practices is that they must be designed to suit the particular context, the particular learning purposes and the particular kind of learners who will be involved. The challenge in using peer learning approaches is to adapt general approaches to ones own needs while retaining the key features that are central to the success of each strategy.

References

Anderson, G, Boud, D and Sampson, J (1996) *Learning Contracts: A practical guide,* Kogan Page, London

Boud, D (1995) *Enhancing Learning through Self Assessment,* Kogan Page, London

Boud, D and Miller, N (eds) (1996) *Working with Experience: Animating learning,* Routledge, London

Boud, D, Cohen, R and Walker, D (eds) (1993) *Using Experience for Learning,* SRHE & Open University Press, Buckingham

Boud, D, Keogh, R and Walker, D (eds) (1985) *Reflection: Turning experience into learning.* Kogan Page, London

Brookfield, S (1986) *Understanding and Facilitating Adult Learning,* Open University Press, Buckingham

Brookfield, S (1990) *The Skillful Teacher: On technique, trust, and responsiveness in the classroom,* Jossey-Bass, San Francisco

Brown, G (1978) *Lecturing and Explaining,* Methuen, London

Brown, G and Hatton, N (1982) *Explanations and Explaining: A teaching skills workbook,* Macmillan Educational, Basingstoke

Brownell, J (1986) *Building Active Listening Skills,* Prentice-Hall Inc, Englewood Cliffs NJ

Chambers, B and Pettman, J (1986) *Anti-racism: A handbook for adult educators,* Australian Government Publishing Service, Canberra

Cornelius, H and Faire, S (1989) *Everyone Can Win: How to resolve conflict,* Simon & Schuster, Sydney

Crum, TF (1987) *The Magic of Conflict: Turning a life of work into a work of art,* Simon & Schuster, New York

Eitington, JE (1996) *The Winning Trainer: Winning ways to involve people in learning,* 3rd edn, Gulf, Houston

Falchikov, N (1995) Peer feedback marking: developing assessment, *Innovation in Education and Training International,* **32** (2), pp 175–87

Falchikov, N (2001) *Learning Together: Peer tutoring in higher education,* Routledge, London

Fulwiler, T (ed) (1987) *The Journal Book,* Heinemann, Portsmouth NH.

Galbraith, M (ed) (1990) *Facilitating Adult Learning: A transactional process,* Krieger, Melbourne FL

Gillespie, J, Guthrie, S, Kelly, S and Sampson, J (1992) *Negotiating Learning in Adult Education* (video), Summer Hill Films, Surry Hills, NSW

Habeshaw, S, Gibbs, G and Habeshaw, T (1987) *53 Interesting Things to do in your Seminars and Tutorials,* 2nd edn, Technical & Educational Services, Bristol

Hayes, E and Colin, S (eds) (1994) *Confronting Sexism and Racism: New directions for adult and continuing education* No. 61, Jossey-Bass, San Francisco

Heron, J (1989) *The Facilitators' Handbook,* Kogan Page, London

Heron, J (1993) *Group Facilitation,* Kogan Page, London

Heron, J (1999) *The Complete Facilitator's Handbook,* Kogan Page, London

Holly, ML (1989) *Writing to Grow: Keeping a personal-professional journal,* Heinemann, Portsmouth NH

Jaques, D (2000) *Learning in Groups,* 3rd edn, Kogan Page, London

Johnson, DW and Johnson, FP (1997) *Joining Together: Group theory and group skills,* 6th edn, Allyn & Bacon, Boston

Jones, K (1991) *Icebreakers: A sourcebook of games, exercises and simulations for trainers and teachers,* Kogan Page, London

Knights, S (1985) Reflection and learning: the importance of a listener, in *Reflection: Turning experience into learning* (eds) D Boud, R Keogh and D Walker, Kogan Page, London

Knowles, M (1975) *Self-Directed Learning: A guide for learners and teachers,* Association Press, New York

Newstrom, J and Scannell, E (1980) *Games Trainers Play,* McGraw Hill, New York

Newstrom, J and Scannell, E (1983) *More Games Trainers Play,* McGraw Hill, New York

Newstrom, J and Scannell, E (1994) *Even More Games Trainers Play,* McGraw Hill, New York

Newstrom, J and Scannell, E (1998) *The Big Book of Team Building Games: Trust building activities, team spirit exercises and other fun things to do,* McGraw Hill, New York

Rainer, T (1980) *The New Diary,* Angus & Robertson, London

Reinertsen, P and Wells, M (1993) Dialogue, journals and critical thinking, *Teaching Sociology,* **21,** pp 182–86

Robinson, J, Saberton, S and Griffin, V (1985) *Learning Partnerships: Interdependent learning in adult education,* Ontario Institute for Studies in Education, Toronto

Scannell, E and Newstrom, J (1991) *Still More Games Trainers Play,* McGraw Hill, New York

Smith, B and Delahaye, B (1998) *How to be an Effective Trainer: Skills for managers and new trainers,* 3rd edn, Wiley, New York

Tiberius, R (1999) *Small Group Teaching: A troubleshooting guide,* Kogan Page, London

Woods, D (1994) *Problem-based Learning: How to gain the most from PBL,* Waterdown, Ontario: Woods. Internet version at http://chemeng.mcmaster.ca

4

Implementing and managing peer learning

Ruth Cohen and Jane Sampson

We have already seen how the process of including peer learning activities enhances student learning and prepares students and graduates for the workplace. These benefits include working with others, managing learning and learning how to learn, developing communication skills and building confidence through self and peer assessment. The chapter on design highlighted the importance of integrating peer learning into the course as a consciously organized and legitimate educational experience. This chapter is concerned with the next stage – the practicalities of implementing and managing it. As a consequence it deals with staff and student issues arising from a changed approach to teaching and learning and includes suggestions for making the process a satisfying and worthwhile experience for staff and students.

Many of the activities practised in peer learning are not new or indeed unique. What is different is the purposeful and systematic approach taken by teachers to include peer learning in the design and implementation of courses and then monitor the process of these activities as well as the outcomes. Additionally, what marks the difference between a more traditional teacher-directed approach and peer learning is that in peer learning students take a more active role in planning and managing their own learning.

With peer learning, the more transparent and planned the processes for students, the more effective and satisfying their experience is likely to be. A number of contextual factors need to be taken into account, which have been identified in earlier chapters. The overall context in which the peer learning activities are introduced is relevant. Broader contextual factors may also include the assumptions students and staff bring and the values of the institution. The learning approaches students are familiar with will relate back to school situations as well as prior higher education courses.

The more immediate contextual factors influencing students' acceptance of peer learning include the learning outcomes expected of the course, their prior experience of group work and collaborative activities (particularly their perception of whether it was successful and how fairly it was assessed). Practical issues such as availability of time and place for learning, and how the course will be assessed also influence acceptance. Of course, the totality of the workload on students can often be the most important factor. If students feel overwhelmed already the suggestion of any additional activity will be rejected.

For teaching staff, prior experience using peer learning is a critical factor as well as expectations of our role as a teacher and what we consider constitutes suitable course assessment and evaluation. Teachers may also be concerned about how this approach fits with the culture of their department: will their colleagues be accepting of what they are doing; will this matter?

With the increasingly complex structure of courses and the different teaching roles now expected of staff, course designers have found it necessary to be very explicit about teaching and learning processes. The major aspects of a course (the context, underpinning philosophy, objectives, content outcomes, resources, teaching and learning processes and the assessment tasks) need to be clearly relevant for developing the required skills and competencies and obviously congruent with each other. This creates fewer dilemmas for students, particularly when they recognize how the different parts of a course cohere in relation to expectations, learning methods and assessment. It is pointless to promote the values of peer learning and expect cooperation from students if, for example, the assessment tasks are norm-referenced examinations. But by embedding peer learning as integral to the course, this approach is legitimized as part of the regular student experience and preparation for work.

From our own experience and that illustrated by the case studies of different disciplines later in this book, it is clear that implementation and management of the teaching and learning processes is critical. In the main, teachers familiar with student-directed learning, self-directed learning, negotiated learning and peer and self-assessment do not find peer learning very different from the teaching approach used in these other student-centred approaches. They are accustomed to careful briefing of students prior to them engaging in such learning activities. For teachers new to this approach, we suggest that time is formally allocated to preparing students to engage in peer learning through orientation, rehearsal and discussion of the processes. These provide the keys to successful implementation.

This chapter is concerned with the practicalities of implementing and managing the peer learning process. We identify four main phases in the process of establishing and maintaining peer learning and discuss the key issues occurring at each phase. The first phase relates to how the teacher prepares to implement peer learning and includes issues such as what teachers need to know, providing a rationale, developing guidelines for students, and preconditions for fostering peer learning. The second phase concerns orienting students to the peer-learning approach. The third phase deals with the role of teachers in the ongoing managing and monitoring of peer learning while the fourth phase develops the theme of students evaluating the outcomes of their peer learning. This chapter then considers problems that might arise for students and finally the impact of peer learning on staff.

While each phase has its own issues, the preparation and orientation phases are critical for getting started and what occurs during these phases impacts on the ability of students to manage and evaluate their own peer learning.

Phase 1. Preparing for peer learning

The preparation phase involves teachers considering the issues involved in the course, deciding which peer learning strategy will be used, preparing documentation for students and planing how they will orient students to peer learning.

There are four key elements to be considered prior to the effective introduction of peer learning.

Staff knowledge

For many students peer learning is an unfamiliar approach, seemingly at odds with their experience of more individual approaches to learning. In order to promote peer learning enthusiastically and convincingly, teaching staff need to be genuinely supportive of the principles underpinning peer learning. Teachers are better able to promote peer learning in their own departments and even more widely if they feel confident of their knowledge and ability to implement and manage the approach, and have had successful experiences with their students. Particular attention needs to be paid to how peer learning will contribute to the outcomes expected to result from the course. Students may respond cynically to the introduction of peer learning as an unnecessary addition to an already overloaded course, unless we can convey specific benefits for them.

Teachers new to this approach but confident about their skills in facilitating student learning may only require informal induction and some helpful hints from more experienced colleagues. A range of peer learning approaches is included in detail in the previous chapter. As suggested in Chapter 5, the links between peer learning and assessment must be addressed.

However, for many staff there may be significant unanticipated changes. Often these relate to prior perceptions of their role in the management of the teaching and learning processes, and there may be implications that manifest themselves when peer learning is a significant part of the course which affect our self-concept and identity as teachers. Specific challenges to the teacher's role will be discussed in a later section.

Providing a rationale

As teachers we need to be able to articulate clearly the educational reasons for introducing this approach. When students are faced with an unfamiliar teaching and learning method they are likely to be appropriately sceptical and disbelieving. They want to know 'what's in it for me' in terms of their broader education and the demands of the course in which they are enrolled. Both short-term learning benefits for this course as well as the benefits for the workplace need to be addressed. Like other group-learning strategies, preparing students for peer learning carries with it responsibility for introducing the processes in a meaningful way. We cannot overestimate the importance of providing a compelling rationale both for the use of peer learning in general and for the particular strategies chosen.

Students have the right to an explanation of how their peer learning will benefit them and why peer learning is integral to their particular course. They would also expect to learn about how this approach fits with academic expectations and future workplace needs and how it relates to the assessment criteria. In our own situation, students working and studying concurrently often observe that the teamwork skills relevant for successful peer learning in class settings are exactly those they need in their work situations, particularly for promotion to more senior positions. Our follow-up evaluations have resulted in students becoming even more positive about their past peer learning experiences, in particular valuing the self-management and communication skills acquired.

Staff should be prepared to devote time to addressing and discussing these concerns and should be willing to modify the procedures, where sensible, in response to issues students raise. Otherwise there is a danger that this approach will be seen simply as a rationalization for diminishing resources in higher education, rather than having intrinsic educative value. If staff cannot give clear and convincing explanations of why the particular use of peer learning is worthwhile for the specific students in question, then they should not consider using these strategies.

Developing guidelines for students

In our experience, documentation in the form of guidelines for students is very useful, and acts as a continuing resource for the duration of the peer learning. The main purpose is to make clear what is expected and to give some examples of how peer learning might work in this particular course. Such guidelines might include a chart identifying all the demands of the course, indicating how the peer learning work complements the workload and assessment tasks. It should show that the time devoted to peer learning is a realistic estimate and has been determined in conjunction with all other expectations.

This documentation shows how peer learning fits with the course. It explains the purpose, the form of peer learning to be used and how students will work together. It does not shy away from possible contentious issues that may emerge and thus provides a valuable resource for students that can be referred to from time to time.

Guidelines commonly provide tips on how to get started and bonding exercises to help groups or partners to be comfortable working together. It may provide a range of learning activities. Guidelines may also have notes on implications of rotating roles in the group, information on group development, suggestions for deciding how to divide the tasks, time management issues, listening skills, questioning skills, feedback ideas, perhaps some reflection and self-evaluation strategies.

The guidelines may propose workshop activities that can be used to help the groups/pairs get started. While their main purpose is to alert students to what is expected of them, they may discuss situations that commonly arise and how they might be dealt with. They may provide scenarios with critical incidents for groups or partners to work through and suggest a debriefing schedule to be used following their deliberations. Similarly, it may be helpful to include material on how groups develop from the forming, storming stages through to formally disbanding the group at the end of the course (for example, Tuckman and Jensen, in Jaques, 2000). Examples of possible tensions and issues that could emerge along the way can be very reassuring so that students can structure their peer learning activities effectively, but if difficulties arise groups are forewarned. Providing examples of real situations and previous students' reflections on how these were handled enable students new to these learning methods to feel more confident about the unfamiliar territory.

We always make clear that these are guidelines rather than instructions, designed to clarify issues and minimize stress in using a new approach. Once started on their tasks, most peer learning groups prefer to develop in their own way. Discussions and debates about how to proceed have their own intrinsic learning value. At the end of each course students have an opportunity to make suggestions about what was helpful and identify other issues to be addressed in the guidelines.

Much of the documentation can be extracted from this book and particularly in the examples from the different disciplines. It is important that in addition to the general guidelines about the particular strategy to be used, students are given local, course specific documentation which addresses matters such as learning outcomes, schedules, deadlines and what each group or pair is required to produce.

Preconditions for fostering peer learning

Peer learning will be more effective if certain conditions are established as part of the culture of the course. Identifying and encouraging these is an important part of student orientation, and we suggest that the orientation process for students include activities that draw attention to them. Of course, it is rare for all of these preconditions to be fulfilled at the early stages of any peer learning activity; some aspects will grow to fruition during the peer learning process. But it is important to put them on the orientation agenda, and that means teachers will have decided on some strategies for introducing these as part of the course.

These preconditions apply whether peer learning takes place in partnerships or small groups. While group learning may appear a more complex activity due to the number of students involved, the intensity of working with only one other creates its own set of issues.

Desirable conditions for fostering peer learning are:

- there is perceived value in cooperation and the roles involved;
- there is a microclimate of trust that already exists or can be established;
- student and staff expectations are discussed;
- there is a basic process that has been agreed on and some initial preparation;
- reflection and reflective discussions are encouraged;
- it is acceptable to make mistakes and seek assistance;
- previous negative experiences with similar activities are discussed and acknowledged with practical suggestions for how to change.

Not all of these can be addressed at the orientation stage. Students themselves should be encouraged to work on them during the initial stages of their meetings.

Phase 2. Orienting students to peer learning

As we have suggested above, time needs to be spent familiarizing students with peer learning activities and processes. This orientation can take place in normal classes or in a specially organized training workshop, depending on the kind of peer learning activities chosen, time available, and the experience students have in working co-operatively. An important goal of the orientation process is for students to gain confidence in using the peer learning processes.

The key features of an orientation session are:

- introducing students to the notions of learning with and from each other;
- modelling/illustrating how these learning processes are consistent with the outcomes of the course;
- demonstrating how to build upon student experiences and use them as a resource for further learning;
- convincing students that different perspectives have validity;
- providing opportunity for doubts and concerns to be raised;
- encouraging sharing in competitive courses;
- information on group development;
- providing a practice session on a relevant topic to try out some of the processes to be used in a safe environment.

A very useful orientation workshop idea is to include students who have already been involved in satisfying peer learning experiences. They can (hopefully) provide enthusiastic accounts of their experiences and outcomes, anticipated and unanticipated, and also relate some of the dilemmas they faced and how these were (or were not) resolved. These students may be pressed to reveal what would have improved the experience, useful information for both students and teachers. Nothing can compare with the persuasive qualities of authentic student accounts of peer learning.

Students find it helpful if teachers can link peer learning in the formal course setting with the informal ways of working together that students are likely to have used in the past. An orientation session provides an opportunity for students to reflect on past learning situations (both formal and informal cooperative learning experiences) in a range of settings. Sharing their thoughts in small groups may be a useful starting point. Articulating what went well and/or how their learning experience might have been improved will assist students to make the most of the new peer learning activities. A well-planned two-hour orientation session can address all the key features listed above and give students an opportunity to engage in one or two short activities. A longer orientation workshop gives a student the opportunity to engage in a number of different activities with a variety of peers before moving to their permanent group or pair, allocated by the teacher or self-selected, and beginning their tasks.

If there is no opportunity for a separate orientation workshop, allocating defined class time in one or two classes to discuss the issues and rehearse a peer learning activity is likely to be useful. A structured 20-minute session can achieve quite a lot. Formally facilitating such peer learning activities acknowledges the importance accorded to the process by the teacher and these events provide a shared experience to which students and staff can refer. Using a controversial topic or even having groups negotiate a topic or decide a process for their peer learning activity may highlight issues inclined to emerge in an unmonitored session. For example, creating a situation in which behaviours such as domination, cynicism or withdrawal may occur, can raise issues that students will meet when they are on their own. Such incidents give staff the opportunity to encourage students to deal directly with their peers rather than use avoidance strategies or seek staff intervention. It may be helpful for students to determine a code of conduct for themselves. As teachers we also need to have a range of strategies available for dealing with such behaviours.

Reflection on the experience (however short or incomplete) may lead students to identify generic skills such as negotiation or communication that can be developed through such group activities. Students could be asked to write a short learning journal entry on their experience as a way of introducing this process. Using a debriefing activity at the end of the peer learning session will provide a model that students can use in their own peer learning sessions.

Peer learning groups established in the orientation session as trial groups may become permanent as the group starts to bond and form a cohesive unit, or they may be limited to the orientation sessions. Where classes are highly complex in character, peer learning groups are more commonly selected by the teacher (as in Chapters 7 and 9) to ensure equity and diversity of participants. Others use random selection.

The importance of this orientation phase cannot be underestimated. It gives students an opportunity to articulate and clarify the rationale behind peer learning and value the importance of learning with each other. It should equip students to begin planning their learning activities, work cooperatively as a team, and provide tips to manage the tasks in the time allocated. At the same time, the potential for enhancing the academic outcomes of the course through opportunities to engage in debate, critical enquiry, sharing resources and reflection is clearly articulated. We need to engage students in substantial dialogue about how particular forms of peer learning can help them with aspects of their work they believe to be important. The orientation event should also deal with such practicalities as arranging times and locations for students to meet, in or out of class, and provision of resources, such as computers, photocopying or whatever is relevant. It may sometimes be appropriate for students to meet and communicate in ways other than face-to-face, such as using the Internet, as in Chapters 10 and 11.

Phase 3. Managing, monitoring and sustaining the events of peer learning

Following orientation, students take control of the situation and develop their own plans for meeting their academic and personal goals. They begin to work together. During this phase students engage in managing their own learning and pursue different ways of learning how to learn. They may seek reassurance about what they are doing and whether the processes they engage in are appropriate. Students more experienced in peer learning are unlikely to involve staff unless they have issues they absolutely cannot resolve themselves.

Students take on the tasks of peer learning, but responsibility for implementing and managing peer learning is still the responsibility of academic staff in the same way as the organization and presentation of subject content are their responsibility. Teachers can monitor the process through observations, chats with students, formal or informal group reports, reading students' reflective journal entries (or their summaries of them if students prefer to keep them confidential), or self or peer assessment by the students. Teaching staff may require partners or groups to provide periodic written reports on their progress which identify tasks completed, analyse the success of their strategies and highlight unresolved issues. For staff the key issue is whether to intervene when progress towards the goals is insufficient and/or personal difficulties have been disclosed, or whether to leave it to the group to rectify the situation.

Students need to be confident that peer learning has the support of staff with a deep understanding of the processes and issues that commonly occur.

By implementing the peer learning activities we are formalizing what would be a highly unpredictable and selective process if left to students and their casual conversations outside the classroom and at the same time making the process more inclusive. We need to manage the learning process in ways that draw upon the best features of teaching and learning, without being overly intrusive. Much of the value of these strategies for learners comes from trying new approaches, standing in the shoes of others and learning about themselves. Success does not mean that meetings are free of conflict or the absence of contentious issues – in many cases dealing with such issues leads to greater learning through students having to deal with these matters. The key to successful peer learning lies in the mutually supportive environment which learners themselves construct and performance of tasks which are relevant to the course of study they are undertaking.

Students unused to being responsible for initiating the planning, managing, assessing and evaluating of their own learning may seek staff confirmation and reviews of their progress at different stages of their learning tasks. They may find it useful to articulate and agree on the code of conduct for the group or pair and to discuss how they might approach any conflict situations or ethical issues that arise. Staff usually find they take a more active role early in the students' use of peer learning but the need for support and/or intervention diminishes as students become more confident of the process. When students continue their peer learning activities into a second semester (often in a different student group/pair) our experience indicates that most are very keen, are quicker in establishing the group norms and take far less time to get into the tasks.

Students' experience of peer learning seems to make them more confident about their capacity to benefit from additional peer learning events. We also find they are better able to cope with uncertainty. Many students also appear more experimental and prepared to take risks in their approaches to defining roles, confronting conflict, working out the power relationships, taking on different roles to facilitate the learning activities, engaging in peer feedback and assessment, and using reflection as a learning device. It is as if their first experience is a rehearsal for the real event.

In many of our courses we timetable a short session early in the semester (usually after three weeks) for sharing accounts of how the peer learning is progressing and to provide an occasion for students to reflect on their own roles in the process. It raises awareness of the importance of keeping track of deadlines. We have found students express greater interest in pursuing their peer learning activities after they discuss what is happening in their own group in an open forum and have the opportunity to find out how other groups are managing. There is some comfort in discovering that your dilemmas are common to other groups. Sharing the processes used and discussing issues that emerged, particularly in the early stages of the implementation, dispels false notions and unrealistic expectations and at the same time provides a context in which to raise important generic or specific concerns. There is always the potential that this process will reveal that a group has been unable to establish a workable relationship and we need to think about how we might address this. Depending on how serious the problem is teachers can suggest ways to reduce the tension, assist with planning, actively intervene in a dispute or even change the membership of the group. Changing group membership is a last resort, as it is likely to have implications for other working groups.

One of the most rewarding aspects of initiating peer learning is when learning partners and even some study groups decide at the end of a course to continue working together, having found the whole experience personally and educationally supportive. Staff members might suggest this as worthwhile, even when students are doing different courses. Sometimes students just need someone in whom they can confide and an opportunity to test ideas. It is not necessary for students to be in the same subject area for peer learning to operate, learning partnerships can continue to flourish using the acquired skills of questioning, rehearsing ideas, giving feedback and using reflection as tools of engagement. A naïve question can draw out responses that clarify how well a student understands concepts and is able to articulate them.

Phase 4. Evaluating outcomes

There are a number of relevant ways of evaluating the outcomes of peer learning, but their timing is critical. Evaluation is an ongoing process – it is of little benefit to students if evaluations are only done at the end of the course. Accessing this sort of data early in a semester gives staff and students the opportunity to make appropriate adjustments. As with assessment, the type of evaluation needs to be in keeping with peer learning philosophy. Several evaluation approaches stand out as being congruent with peer learning goals:

- Self-evaluations: Evaluations by an individual student critically reviewing his/her own learning, based on personally determined goals and criteria established earlier in the course. The most common method used to document this information is the reflective learning journal (Boud, in press). As the written material in a journal is generally regarded as confidential, students are encouraged to select several items they are willing to make public and document these for others to see. Or they may choose to discuss some of their highlights and concerns with a staff member or learning partner. Other useful approaches include 'the letter to myself' or using metaphors to analyse the process and its outcomes.

- Group or pair evaluations. Evaluations by peers on their joint outcomes – using criteria specific to the group/pair or that determined by students and staff for the whole class. The discussion that precedes the documentation is the most important part of this process, as the agreed written précis is usually rather general in order to meet everyone's requirements. Using small group feedback sessions can also elucidate vital information in order to raise the quality of the learning experiences. Students can provide evaluative statements or respond to particular questions anonymously on small pieces of paper which are later distributed at random and read out, so all the information is public, but the authorship is confidential. Alternatively, hang charts with headings such as 'what works''what I want changed' and 'other comments' and students can write Post-it notes and place them on a board. This is relatively private but provides a way of eliciting and displaying honest responses.

- Staff evaluations. These are evaluations of the outcomes of the group/pair as part of the normal evaluation process, but including some criteria nominated by the students. Staff may use standard form evaluations or more creative approaches such as drawings, poems or song in which groups develop performance pieces in a very short time that identify critical themes. Interviews with students also provide valuable data. Rating scales on their own are unlikely to provide the qualitative data needed, but may be useful if combined with the space for students to comment.

The outcomes of the evaluation need to be visible – that is, students want evidence of how their comments have been influential in reinforcing what exists or bringing in modifications to the peer learning process. Positive evaluations by students are likely to influence other teachers to use peer learning activities in their courses. We would encourage teachers to use staff seminars, conferences, and publishing to discuss and promote their peer learning approaches and provide evidence of the outcomes. There is considerable opportunity for further qualitative research in this area.

What problems might arise for students?

The single most potent problem arising in peer learning is associated with issues of difference. If students do not accept each other as peers, then much of the discussion on peer learning is irrelevant because it is based on the assumption that students will act as if they were. When they do not, difficulties arise.

The kinds of differences that appear to influence how groups and pairs perform together include those of gender, local versus overseas students, culture and religion as well as differences in knowledge and experience bases. Oppressive behaviour by dominant group members can and does occur. When these differences compound, difficulties can arise if the issues are not addressed explicitly. Ways of dealing with some of these issues are discussed in Chapter 3. It is vital they get addressed in every setting, not least because students are being prepared to work in a diverse society and if university courses do not prepare students to use the benefits of difference, we are not discharging our wider responsibilities. In these circumstances we are acting to reinforce patterns of oppression.

Despite evidence to the contrary, students do not often report their issues as relating to difference. Sometimes it is because it is not recognized as such, but subsumed into other areas of concern. It may also be because it is seen as politically difficult. Our experience suggests that the major problems students make public relate to difficulties adjusting to the new approaches, difficulties in the group and their confusion about the role of the teacher.

Orientation provides a shared introductory experience with the rationale for using peer learning. If students miss the orientation, or for some reason fail to gain a sufficient understanding of the purpose of the peer learning, it may take considerable time before they readjust their teaching and learning concepts to take advantage of this approach effectively.

A dilemma for students is the change in the anticipated roles of teachers and students. Peer learning confronts their perception of the traditional roles and then expects students to adjust quickly to the new roles. Some students, although not necessarily the older students who have gained much of their learning through experience, find it difficult to cope with these changes. They expect teachers to control all learning through teaching. Others who are familiar with student-centred learning may become irritated at the difficulties that some students find adjusting to their new role. Where there are parallel classes engaged in peer learning activities, students are often aware and annoyed by the different approaches (for example, assistance with resources, academic advice) taken by the teaching staff.

Another student issue in peer learning relates to their control of the process. There are inevitable power plays, students not taking their responsibilities seriously and problems within groups. Freeloaders create problems, but students do not always feel confident to confront them. Sometimes leadership issues emerge. If group-based peer learning is used, then an understanding of basic group dynamics and group development is important in helping address the issues that inevitably occur (see, for example Jaques, 2000; Tiberius, 1999). This knowledge enables them to better recognize the processes and understand why different tensions emerge. Students can see that some issues arise not as a result of their own deficiencies, but are normal and common occurrences in any group of people working on a task.

A further area leading to tensions within the group emerges from the different values held by individuals and their different ways of working and time management. This may well be the first time students have had to rely on the work of another student as part of their own output. Students have rarely had access to the work of other students so it is often a surprise for them to find that students differ in their views on what comprises appropriate quality and amount of work to fulfil a given task. These issues need to be discussed and some protocols established.

With peer learning, students become joint directors of their own learning that may include designing relevant and personally useful curriculum, determining the content and processes for the learning and developing tools to assess and evaluate outcomes. Peer learning also provides important opportunities for collaborative decision making, such as deciding with whom to work, how to manage the learning tasks and how to accommodate the preferred learning approaches of others. For students accustomed to being individually responsible in a teacher–directed situation, these can be profound and disturbing changes.

Some examples of real issues that students face include the following. A number can be eliminated if the orientation process identifies these as areas requiring attention, and students have an opportunity to discuss and rehearse their responses to such issues. Encouraging students to develop explicit codes of conduct for their group/pair often provides the opportunity to raise these issues hypothetically before they become troubling. It is hardly surprising that most of these issues do not relate to academic course matters but rather the people aspects of peer learning:

- different expectations in groups by gender such as female students expected to take notes for the male-dominated group (the secretary role for women);
- tensions/different expectations of local and overseas students;
- students being indecisive and unable to commit to the topic for a student-led workshop;
- students unwilling to provide feedback or students unwilling to accept feedback;
- decision making not equitable;

- decisions made without consultation;
- students who do not contribute their share of work;
- dominant students unwilling to listen;
- time wasters, procrastinators;
- changes in group membership during the course;
- students who suffer severe traumas and invite 'therapy' from their groups.

There are a number of additional examples in the case study chapters.

Impact of peer learning on staff

There are also significant changes for teaching staff when they introduce peer learning to their students.

The changes in the role of teaching staff as a result of the implementation of peer learning should not be underestimated. For some staff these changes will be a matter of degree only; for others this approach will be a major change. The change from a teacher-directed approach, in which all decisions about teaching and learning are made by the teacher, to a more student-centred approach, in which learning is negotiated with students (and perhaps even between the students themselves), will need some supportive strategies. The potential loss of control over aspects of the subject or course may affect staff self-image.

Staff development is an integral part of the change process. Working with student-led groups, negotiating learning and rethinking what constitutes effective learning and valid assessment procedures means reviewing the course to develop greater congruity between ways of learning and approaches to assessment. Staff members require orientation and skills for managing peer learning situations that commonly arise. While their teaching role may differ, there is no abdication of responsibility for the students.

The issue of assessment is of concern to many staff unaccustomed to qualitative assessment procedures. Peer learning provides an opportunity to rethink assessment procedures and to develop alternative approaches to traditional quantitative assessment models. Developing a deeper understanding of the importance of peer learning is likely to be strengthened if there is serious consideration of the links between these new types of learning activities and traditionally accepted assessment approaches (see Chapter 5).

Staff sometimes find it hard to resist the temptation to intervene too often in the students' activities and discussions in their peer learning activities. Apart from initial guidance, the staff member's role is essentially to ensure that the full learning potential of the exercise is realized. This is unlikely if key decisions are influenced or even determined by staff rather than by students. Staff may suggest some ideas to help a group that is stuck but students are ultimately responsible for their own learning. A staff member is more likely to take the role of mentor or mediator with regard to group processes, rather than assist with traditional subject content. For example, they may be called upon to clarify what is expected of a partnership. In this case it might be helpful to suggest that the partners focus on one personal outcome and one joint outcome with which they would be happy. Or teachers may be asked to suggest some facilitative strategies a group can use to become more inclusive. Knowledge of group processes and group development is a decided advantage for dealing with these complex issues.

Knowing how to recognize conflict in peer groups, when it is appropriate to intervene and how to do so gently, is also part of the new role of staff. There is far greater emphasis on students' experiential and contextual learning, therefore handout materials need to explain the learning strategy, questions and problematic issues, value different approaches and responses, suggest questions rather than simply provide information.

At the end of a course incorporating peer learning there is usually a need for a sensitive formal closure. Students have generally worked together closely and formed very strong bonds, and may be sad (or relieved). It can be a simple event that includes some ritual or ceremonial marker to indicate the end of this phase. For example, a stimulating and engaging way of closing is to use 'photolanguage' (Cooney and Burton, 1986). Photolanguage is a series of 120 black-and-white photographs that cover every aspect of life. Photographs are laid out so all can be seen and students select two or three that they see as best representing their response to a question posed by the teacher. In this case, students might be asked to select pictures that best represent their experience of peer learning. Students then explain briefly why they chose particular pictures to the group. Staff need to be aware that this process can evoke very emotional responses. Or, staff might simply ask students to decide how they will manage the closing ceremony.

This chapter has covered a broad territory, as the process of implementing and managing peer learning is like peeling the onion – there are many layers. The major change from traditional teaching to peer learning is the shift of the locus of responsibility for learning from teacher to student, so these experiences will lead to a capacity for learning how to learn with others in a way which is cohesive, productive and personally satisfying.

References

Boud, D (in press) Using journal writing to enhance reflective practice, in *Journal Writing in Adult Education*, (eds) English, L and Gillen, M, Jossey-Bass, San Francisco

Cooney, J and Burton, K (1986) *Photolanguage Australia – Human Values*, Catholic Education Office, Sydney

Jaques, D (2000) *Learning in Groups*, 3rd edn, Kogan Page, London

Tiberius, R (1999) *Small Group Teaching: A troubleshooting guide*, Kogan Page, London

5

Peer learning and assessment

David Boud, Ruth Cohen and Jane Sampson

Acceptance of peer learning by students, and its ultimate success, often depends upon resolving the question of how peer learning can be assessed in ways that are credible and that also enhance its use. Assessment is the single most powerful influence on learning in formal courses and, if not designed well, can easily undermine the positive features of an important strategy in the repertoire of teaching and learning approaches.

The aim of this chapter is to examine the implications for assessment practice of the adoption of peer learning. It considers situations in which reciprocal peer learning is used as a significant component of a given subject, for example when the tutorial element of a subject is based on peer learning. Our argument emphasizes the importance of congruence between assessment practices and the kinds of learning a course aims to promote. We suggest that the traditional individualistic conception of assessment taken for granted in universities needs to be reassessed if cooperation and collaboration such as that manifest in peer learning is to be fostered.

We start by noting why assessment is a particularly significant issue in the context of peer learning. We then consider the effects of assessment on learning in general before exploring what features of assessment design need to be taken into account. Finally, we identify the kinds of assessment practices to which considerations of this kind lead and end by pointing to issues that need further debate before they can be resolved.

Why assess peer learning?

Assessment needs to be taken into account when considering peer learning for three main reasons:

- *Addressing important educational outcomes.* Peer learning is a process for aiding students in achieving particular learning outcomes, some of which might be pursued in other ways. However, it can also be used to address course goals not readily developed otherwise. These include both course-specific goals, such as those related to professional teamwork, as well as broader goals for lifelong learning. If these outcomes are important, assessment should reflect this.
- *Valuing peer learning.* The presence of formal assessment is often regarded as an indicator of importance. If something is not assessed it can be seen by students and by staff to be of lesser importance than those aspects of a course which are assessed. Students' attention is therefore focused on those course goals that appear to be assessed over others which are not. As peer learning has not previously been highly valued in formal courses, assessment can be a way of indicating the shift of importance.
- *Recognizing commitment.* Assessment can act as a form of academic currency providing compensation for the extra effort that might be involved in undertaking peer learning. Peer learning is often introduced into courses to encourage the pursuit of a wider range of learning outcomes than occurs otherwise, such as those discussed above. If students are expected to put more effort into a course through their engagement in peer learning activities, then it may be necessary to have this effort recognized through a commensurate shift in assessment focus.

An illustration of the influence of assessment can be seen by setting a group of students to work on a specific project. Questions raised often include those about how the project will be assessed and what weighting it might have as part of the overall assessment requirements. In other words, what will it count for? If the weighting is low or if the form of assessment does not appear to acknowledge the expected achievements, then students may be less inclined to take the project seriously.

We believe that it is necessary not only to develop peer learning processes to complement other aspects of teaching and learning, but also to associate assessment with them. It is likely that the more competitive a course is and the greater the focus of student attention on assessment, the more necessary it will be for formal assessment to be associated with peer learning.

However, it is equally important not to use assessment as a device to get students to engage in peer learning activities if they cannot be justified on educational grounds. Assessment should normally follow educational goals and fit with the design of courses, not determine them. It may be necessary to modify assessment processes or drop them if they act to undermine desirable peer learning processes. It is important not to take an excessively instrumental view of assessment, to be sensitive to student views, needs and interests on this and not use assessability as a compliance device.

Having decided that assessment should be associated with peer learning, the question arises: what should be assessed? Should it be peer learning *per se*? And, if so, which aspects? Or should assessment be linked to particular learning outcomes readily promoted through peer learning? There are difficulties in both cases.

Difficulties in assessing peer learning

There are good reasons for linking assessment to peer learning but this should be done with caution:

- *Assessing outcomes related to peer learning may not make students engage more actively in it.* Students already engage in many valuable learning activities in courses without them being directly assessed. The addition of assessment should only occur when it will enhance this engagement and not if it is likely to lead to undesirable consequences, such as encouraging conformity in return for grades.
- *Assessment of peer learning may be more trouble than it is worth.* If peer learning is seen as an everyday aspect of teaching and learning and of intrinsic value, then assessment may not be necessary. An example of this is in the use of learning partnerships in part-time courses for busy professionals. Assessment is not needed because students often find involvement in such partnerships intrinsically satisfying (Robinson, Saberton and Griffin, 1985).
- *Assessment can easily inhibit the processes it is designed to enhance if it is not implemented sensitively.* Peer learning typically pursues learning outcomes traditionally hard to assess, for example those related to group work, oral communication, planning and self-assessment. There is a well-developed repertoire of assessment practices to judge knowledge acquisition, writing skills and problem solving. Indeed, it might be argued that these are overassessed relative to other outcomes in most university courses.

However, peer learning is particularly vulnerable to being affected by inappropriate forms of assessment. The assessment repertoire is less well developed and staff assessment skills less finely honed in areas with which it is most associated. Assessment criteria need to be appropriate for the overall learning outcomes. Some restraint may also be needed in limiting the assessment. If too many things are assessed within a single activity, there is a danger that one or all of them may be devalued. Great care needs to be taken to avoid students automatically assuming that the presence of assessment implies that it is inappropriate to work with others.

Consideration of outcomes of peer learning is an especially useful test for the application of principles of good assessment practice. Because of the vulnerability of peer learning to poor assessment, it provides a good challenge for assessment design.

What are the effects of assessment on learning?

Before turning to the problem of assessment design for peer learning, it is necessary to focus on the effects of assessment on learning generally so that these might be taken into account in developing appropriate policies and processes. The following points summarize a complex literature.

The individual is emphasized

There is a tradition of individual, competitive assessment in most educational institutions even when the notion of competition is not directly espoused. There is a move towards criterion-referenced or competency-based assessment but it is only partial and there are still remnants of an earlier, more explicitly competitive, conception. Norm-referenced assessment implies and requires competition against others rather than cooperation. In an individualistic view of assessment collaboration is regarded as cheating (Kohn, 1992). Assessment is conventionally framed to de-emphasize the collaboration fostered in peer learning.

Assessment exercises power and control over students

Assessment is the principal mechanism whereby staff exercise power and control over students. Assessment practices not only exercise direct influence over students, but promote forms of self-surveillance that discipline students through their own self-monitoring without them even being aware of what is occurring (Edwards and Usher, 1994). Choice, in assessment, is often illusory and the rhetoric of students collaborating for assessment purposes, as might happen in peer learning, is often discouraged through the influence of overriding assessment paradigms. The effect on learning is to circumscribe it to the range of outcomes unilaterally defined as legitimate by staff. Students learn first to distrust their own judgements and then act as agents to constrain themselves.

Assessment exerts a backwash effect on learning

Studies of students' experiences of learning have drawn attention to the strong influences that assessment practices have on their approaches to learning (Marton, Hounsell and Entwistle, 1997). Inappropriate forms of assessment appear to encourage students to take a surface approach to learning. That is, students focus on rote learning, conforming to the narrowest interpretations of assessment tasks and working to 'beat the system' rather than engage in meaningful learning. If such forms of assessment are used in a peer learning context, then cooperation will ensure the rapid spread of instrumental approaches to learning.

Overload of tasks discourages deep approaches to learning

In a similar manner, courses that students perceive as overloaded also contribute to students taking a surface approach to learning tasks (Ramsden and Entwistle, 1981). This has considerable implications if peer assessment is used as a supplement to courses in ways that add to the overall study burden on students, rather than as a substitute for other forms of teaching and learning activity. Overloading is likely to lead peer learning activities either to be ignored or to fall into disrepute.

Assessment practices need to be matched to outcomes

The matching of assessment approaches to desired learning outcomes is at present taking on a renewed significance. Assessment needs not only to reflect outcomes in a narrow technical sense, but in terms of the basic knowledge, understanding, communicative and competency aims which are being pursued in a course (Brew, 1995). As discussed earlier, the desired learning outcomes promoted by peer learning must feature strongly in assessment tasks.

Formal assessment processes should encourage self-assessment

Assessment in higher education has a dual function of judging for the purpose of providing credentials and for the purpose of improving learning. As far as the latter purpose is concerned, assessment should leave students better equipped to engage in their own self-assessments. Unless assessment fosters this, it acts to undermine an important goal of lifelong learning (Boud 1995a).

Consideration of findings such as these leads to the need to design assessment processes carefully so as to avoid the many unintended and negative consequences.

What features of assessment design need to be taken into account for peer learning?

In a paper on the need for assessment practices to promote desired forms of learning, Boud (1995b) identified a number of issues that need to be addressed if assessment is to meet the challenge of enhancing rather than undermining learning. Some of these are presented here and critical questions for the design of assessment are raised.

Focusing on key outcomes

Assessment needs to focus on the central outcomes desired as part of education for a given discipline, field or profession and engage with the most important concepts and practices valued in the course framework. Clarity about the particular outcomes sought from the use of peer learning must be obtained before assessment activities are designed. If the emphasis is on using peer learning to improve subject-matter learning, it will lead to one kind of assessment design. If the emphasis is on promoting teamwork then design for assessment will need to be quite different.

Holistic design

One of the main traps of assessment design is to create an array of assessment techniques each of which may be suitable for assessing different outcomes, but which, when put together, have a different effect altogether. This is a particular danger in the assessment of peer learning. Given that, in many situations, peer learning will only form part of a course, it is likely that familiar and conventional forms of assessment that apply to the other part will tend to dominate perceptions of staff and students. For assessment to be holistic, emphasis needs to be given to the strategy and process of what is required to achieve the specific result. Assessment tasks that engage learners in the whole of a process rather than in fragments should be considered so that the activities of peer learning are not inadvertently marginalized. Holistic design also needs to ensure that staff and students interpret assessment tasks in the same way. If they do not, then they are not working towards the same ends.

Taking account of consequences

Assessment must always be judged in terms of its consequence on student learning, both intended and unintended. The question to be asked is: does assessment act to encourage quality learning (deep/meaningful approaches to study) and discourage undesired learning practices (short-term memorizing for tests, avoidance of collaboration)? When peer learning is used, the question is also: how can assessment activities support meaningful engagement by students in the learning activities being promoted?

Contributing to lifelong learning development

The range of assessment tasks in a course should leave students better equipped to engage in continuing learning and their own self-assessment. If peer learning explicitly and effectively pursues lifelong learning outcomes such as working with others, planning and organizing learning, moving beyond dependence and independence to interdependence this criterion should be met, so long as assessment focuses on these.

Using appropriate language and assumptions

Avoidance of 'final vocabulary' (Rorty, 1989) is especially important in assessment related to peer learning. That is, abstract judgemental vocabulary is excluded and feedback is given about particular task-related accomplishments. Care also needs to be taken that assumptions are not made about the subject matter or the learners that are irrelevant to the task and that are differentially perceived by different groups of students.

Promoting a self-reflexive view of assessment practice

Peer-learning activities have an advantage over other teaching and learning strategies in that they have considerable potential to promote critical reflection.

Critical reflection can focus on the topics considered, the assessment activities themselves and the peer learning processes in which participants are engaged. They can do this if sufficient attention is given to the creation of a climate for learning and assessment that encourages reciprocal communication and openness to feedback.

Not all of these features can be encompassed in every assessment task, or indeed every subject, but they provide a yardstick against which assessment practices compatible with peer learning can be judged.

To what kinds of practices do considerations of this kind lead?

To assess validly the collaborative outcomes of reciprocal peer learning requires an approach differing from traditional methods that rely on assessment as a means of ranking students. Ranking, or rather the anticipation of ranking, is a sure way to inhibit cooperation. Whether the goal of peer learning is developing conceptual understanding or attitudinal change, the criteria for judgement needs to be first accepted by the group of peers. This may involve either criteria determined by them, negotiated with a staff adviser, or proposed by an adviser and agreed to by students. From these criteria, assessment activities can be directed at determining what sort of outcomes, if any, have resulted.

While acknowledging the need for substantial development of a range of strategies for assessment of peer learning, it is possible to point to some examples and identify strengths and weaknesses of each. We focus here on strategies taken partly from the literature and partly from our own practice. They are group assessment, peer feedback and self-assessment, assessment of process, negotiated assessment and the use of cumulative rather than weighted assessment. In many of these processes students are involved in identifying and/or creating assessment criteria. This is particularly important as it is only through gaining a thorough appreciation of criteria and the ability to apply these to their own work that they can become autonomous learners. Detailed strategies for involving students with assessment criteria are discussed in Boud (1995b). We emphasize here summative assessment – assessment that contributes towards students' recorded performance in a course – as it is this aspect of assessment that often proves to be most problematic in peer learning.

Group assessment

If students are expected to cooperate and work together, the notion of assessing them in terms of group rather than individual outcomes can appear attractive.

Group assessment is justified on the grounds that if teamwork and collaborative learning are valued, this must be reflected in an assessment process that stresses that students are judged on their collective efforts, not those of just any one person. There are many variations on this theme, ranging from situations in which all members of a group are given an identical assessment, to others in which there is a separation of individual assessments for some features and group assessments for others. Another option, designed to prevent freeloading, is to make the group assessment the sum of individual members' assessments. Examples of this approach are discussed later in Chapters 8 and 11.

The unfamiliarity of group assessment can create difficulties. Students are used to being judged in terms of their own efforts and can resent others gaining credit for what they perceive as their own contributions, particularly within the context of a competitive course. Unless there are sufficient opportunities to build group planning and group accountability skills, then the use of group assessment is premature. Schemes in which there is an explicit mix of individual and group assessment for common tasks might provide a bridge to wider use of group assessment in these circumstances (Brew, 1995).

Peer feedback and self-assessment

Our own experience suggests that the use of peer assessment in which students make formal assessments of others within a working group can inhibit cooperation. Students have raised questions about the contradictions between a learning process of working together to help each other and an assessment process that implicitly or explicitly pits one person against another.

However, the input of peers into assessment decisions is valuable and ways of using data of this kind must be found. A useful way of doing this is through an emphasis on self-assessment informed by peers. Peers provide rich information, which is then used by individuals to make their own assessments (Boud, 1995b: 200–06). Peer comments are systematically sought with respect to criteria identified either by the group or the learner. The use of grades, marks or other agglomerations of judgements that are not transparent is avoided in this feedback for the sake of specific information relating to the detailed qualities of the work under consideration.

The balance between self and teacher assessment in any given course is a function of many considerations. As far as peer learning is concerned, the emphasis on the kind of assessment processes discussed here should be directly related to the priority given to peer learning and the specific learning outcomes associated with it.

Assessment of process

An alternative focus on peer learning is to shift the emphasis away from learning outcomes towards learning processes. The assessment of participation in which students' contributions towards the process of learning are rewarded is an example of an assessment practice of this kind (Armstrong and Boud, 1983).

While assessment of knowledge will be very familiar to all students, assessment of process is likely to be new. Assessment may well begin with making judgements about the effectiveness of each phase of the activity. The focus may then shift to consider some specific processes such as leadership, negotiation and conflict management, participant interactions, task perform-ance, provision of feedback and so forth. The insights that emerge from analysing these types of processes and the changes in learning that occurred can then be identified and critiqued within the group and jointly documented as evidence of learning for assessment purposes.

Negotiated assessment

There is considerable scope for the use of negotiated assessments for peer learning. Negotiated assessment involves the parties concerned agreeing on the assessment process in the light of their learning goals, activities and anticipated outcomes, recording the mechanism and criteria of assessment and applying this to their own deliberations (Anderson, Boud and Sampson, 1996). For peer learning, the parties would principally be the learners themselves within any given group, but would normally involve a teacher if the results were to be used for formal assessment. The role of the teacher might be to ensure consistency across groups and to see that non-negotiable criteria applicable to the course were included.

There are many variations on this theme, ranging from individually negotiated learning contracts that take into account group criteria, to fully negotiated group contracts that include individual criteria within them. Deciding which to adopt is a choice based upon the desired learning outcomes being pursued and the acceptability of group agreements for assessment purposes within any given course rules. In some of these approaches there may be a need for some non-negotiable criteria to be included specific to the learning outcomes associated with peer learning.

Negotiated assessment is often needed in order to accommodate the varying opportunities that exist in peer learning to demonstrate performance. It is common in peer learning activities for students to have differentiated roles. Their assessable products may not be the same. Negotiation can vary details of assessment across students to allow equal opportunities for demonstration of desired outcomes.

Use of cumulative rather than weighted assessment

When the weighting of any given element of a course is less than 20 per cent, it can give the message that this aspect is valued very little, and students might be prompted to ignore it or put little energy into it.

One solution is to treat each element of assessment as a prerequisite for completion of a subject or course unit. When this is done, assessment associated with peer learning (and indeed all other elements) can be regarded as 100 per cent of the final assessment as all need to be completed at a satisfactory level before students can be regarded as having completed. For example, participation in a study group, project team or a learning partnership could be integrated into a course in such a way that it is not possible to pass the course without demonstrating such involvement even if no actual marks are awarded for the participation itself.

What issues remain to be addressed?

As in any discussion of assessment, as soon as practices are examined in detail, many issues are raised. Some may pose significant dilemmas in particular contexts. However it is important not to be excessively negative as many of the assessment issues related to peer learning are equally applicable to other forms of assessment and they do not appear to provide insurmountable barriers in those. It is unreasonable to apply higher and more difficult standards to the assessment of peer learning than to traditional, lecturer-directed means of assessment. It is easy to indicate that there may be some difficulties (such as potential freeloaders), but prior to dismissing assessment in the peer learning context it is worth examining whether there is any possibility for students to beat the current system! If the answer is yes, it is not a sufficient reason to neglect the overall value of the assessment of peer learning because there may be some who abuse it. In addition, assessment of peer learning is likely to be an additional learning event, in useful ways that traditional summative testing rarely achieves. If a goal of higher learning is to equip learners for a lifetime of learning and assessment independent of teachers, as we believe it is, then engaging in assessment in conjunction with peer learning provides a useful foundation.

Individual versus group focus

Peer learning has essentially a group focus, whereas assessment in higher education has almost exclusively focused on individuals. It is in this aspect that the greatest challenge exists. There is a danger that assessment of peer learning becomes so tokenistic or so loaded against the kinds of learning outcomes that peer learning promotes that it becomes irrelevant. It is not simply a matter of designing assessment processes to accommodate peer learning. A basic issue to be faced is whether assessment can foster group learning whilst not inhibiting individual achievement. This can be done but it requires a broader view of assessment to be adopted within institutions, a view that does not systematically privilege an individualistic rather than collective orientation. Without this change, severe limits to what is possible in practice will remain.

There are also practical questions to be addressed. These include how the exploiting of peers by unscrupulous students can be avoided. And how can we avoid peer pressure and 'groupthink' (Janis, 1983), which may act to encourage surface approaches or 'beat the system' attitudes? There are no simple solutions to these questions although this book does provide some important strategies. They must be the subject of continual vigilance to ensure they do not become significant problems in any particular context.

Process versus task or product

What should be the balance between assessing process and outcomes? Should there be a balance and how might that be determined in specific contexts? It is perfectly reasonable to use assessment of the process of peer learning as an initial learning phase within a total assessment scheme. Satisfactory experience of process assessment of this kind can lead to students developing confidence in the outcomes of peer learning. This is critical to using peer learning more widely. Assessment of process, task or product will of course necessitate clear criteria being developed.

Perhaps initially, assessment can be conducted with input from the total class. As reasons and explanations are forwarded for awarding specific results, be they on the basis of pass/fail or grading, values and hidden assumptions (old paradigms) are articulated and a greater understanding of the holistic nature and purpose of assessment is likely to emerge. What makes university-level learning can also be raised as a matter to be considered.

New approaches versus traditional assessment

How do new forms of assessment supportive of peer learning relate to the need for marks and grades? Indeed, if marks and grades are not used for peer learning in courses in which they otherwise feature strongly then peer learning may appear to be of lower status than other aspects. One way of developing skills in this area and becoming confident about its use – for both staff and students – may occur where lecturers want to tread cautiously, including peer assessment processes as a requirement for completing the subject but not necessarily attaching a grade to the outcome.

Control versus responsibility

How do we deal with the effects of an oppressive assessment regime that neither staff or students have the power to alter? If course requirements specify a particular form of assessment, incorporating an additional or different element within this specification may prove problematic. There are important aspects of peer learning that probably should not be assessed at risk of destroying them (for example personal reflection, interpersonal relationships). In common with all forms of assessment, peer assessment uses a sampling process – so not all aspects can be assessed all the time. Deciding what to assess is as important as deciding how best to assess it. It is here that some degree of responsibility for assessment must be passed from the lecturer to the learners themselves.

Conclusion

Assessment can foster peer learning, but only if it is consciously planned to be compatible. If peer learning is introduced into a course this should act as an immediate prompt to review assessment practices. It is not possible to think about assessment and peer learning in ways uncontaminated by the issues of power and control central to assessment of students by teachers. Assessment is a highly loaded term with strong connotations and associations for everyone. Where peer learning is used assessments need to at least acknowledge if not reward collaboration. The key concern is not compromising assessment practices for the sake of peer learning, but making assessment tasks friendly to peer learning, through the promotion of positive practices and the avoidance of those that are inhibiting.

There are also implications for curriculum development. As Newble and Jaeger (1983) have noted 'examinations have a massive steering effect on the curriculum' despite the philosophical tendencies of staff using more innovative teaching methods to de-emphasize the role of assessment. It is therefore unrealistic to discuss assessment in isolation from curriculum content and teaching strategies. If peer learning is to play a part in university experience, as we strongly believe it should, ways of assessing its value must be explored together with strategies for its effective implementation. Such an exploration will also raise questions in regard to the assumptions and traditions underpinning other forms of assessment currently in use. This in itself is no bad thing and in some cases probably long overdue.

References

Anderson, G, Boud, D and Sampson, J (1996) *Learning Contracts: A practical guide,* Kogan Page, London

Armstrong, M and Boud, D (1983) Assessing class participation: an exploration of the issues, *Studies in Higher Education,* **8** (1), pp 33–44

Boud, D (1995a) Assessment and learning: contradictory or complementary? In *Assessment for Learning in Higher Education* (ed) P Knight, pp 35–48, Kogan Page, London

Boud, D (1995b) *Enhancing Learning through Self-Assessment,* Kogan Page, London

Brew, A (1995) Self-assessment in different domains, in *Enhancing Learning through Self Assessment* (ed) D Boud, pp 129–54, Kogan Page, London

Edwards, R and Usher, R (1994) Disciplining the subject: the power of competence, *Studies in the Education of Adults,* **26** (1), pp 1–14

Janis, I (1983) *Groupthink,* Houghton Mifflin, Boston

Kohn, A (1992) *No Contest: The case against competition,* Houghton Mifflin, Boston

Marton, F, Hounsell, D and Entwistle, N (eds) (1997) *The Experience of Learning: Implications for teaching and studying in higher education,* 2nd edn, Scottish Academic Press, Edinburgh

Newble, D and Jaeger, K (1983) The effect of assessment and examinations on the learning of medical students, *Medical Education,* **13,** pp 263–68

Ramsden, P and Entwistle, N (1981) Effects of academic departments on students' approaches to studying, *British Journal of Educational Psychology,* **51,** pp 368–83

Robinson, J, Saberton, S and Griffin, V (1985) *Learning Partnerships: Interdependent Learning in Adult Education,* Department of Adult Education, Ontario Institute for Studies in Education, Toronto

Rorty, R (1989) *Contingency, Irony and Solidarity,* Cambridge University Press, Cambridge

Part two

Case studies

6

Team-based learning in management education

Ray Gordon and Robert Connor

This chapter describes our use of team-based learning to teach organizational behaviour to MBA classes. One of the guiding contexts of the subject is the trend in contemporary management towards the widespread adoption of new organizational forms, in particular, structures that focus on empowerment and the creation of more egalitarian work environments. Our adoption of peer learning to supplement tutor-centred teaching was an attempt to promote autonomy in learning (Boud, 1988) as a logical precursor of autonomy at work. Team-based learning programmes provide the learning environment that is most similar to the evolving work environments that students are likely to experience. That is, as Rynes and Trank (1999) suggest, peer learning encourages business students to engage with the less orthodox and rational side of their chosen profession by forcing them to deal with emotional issues, question their assumptions and experiment with new ideas and perspectives.

The peer learning programme and the data it has generated is outlined. We conclude that team-based peer learning programmes can contribute significantly to the development of the knowledge and skills required for people-management roles, but the design of the peer learning programme must reflect the local context in which it is conducted. Thus, a peer learning programme in a business faculty is likely to be very different from one in an education faculty. Furthermore, practitioners relying on the existing peer learning literature, which is valuable for its broad pedagogical guidance, may miss important contextual variables that can produce unexpected outcomes from peer learning programmes.

The context for peer learning

As a foundation unit in the MBA and other postgraduate programmes, our subject, Managing People, typically has a semester enrolment of 250 to 400 students who attend in classes of size 30. Classes are presented by six to eight full-time and adjunct lecturers. In designing the team-based learning approach, we considered two important contextual factors – the widespread adoption of new organizational forms by business in recent years and the changing demographics of our classroom. With respect to the latter, managing people has a high enrolment of international students who bring great diversity to the classroom. A significant percentage of students, including local students, have English as their second language, there is a wide range of academic backgrounds and a broad set of needs, interests, ideologies and learning styles. The often-conflicting nature of these factors has critical implications for teaching generally and peer learning in particular.

Increasing diversity in the classroom echoes some of the changes occurring in organizations today. Advances in technology, particularly information technology, and the shifting nature of economies throughout the world have accelerated the globalization of business and social environments. In consequence the barriers of distance between countries are breaking down resulting in different cultural, ideological and work perspectives being involuntarily thrust together. The potential for misunderstanding and conflict has subsequently heightened as diverse organizations and people are compelled to work together through the widespread use of new organizational forms such as teams as the basic unit of work.

As business environments change, organizations are adopting flatter, more organic forms, which signals a major shift in the relationship between power and control in organizations (Clegg and Hardy, 1996). Such a shift suggests that it is the nature of relationships that is becoming the new controlling mechanism in organizations. As Porter and McKibbin (1988) and Beck (1994) point out, the emerging forms of organization demand the acquisition of the sorts of skills that have traditionally been left to chance – skills that are often described as 'soft' or 'people' skills.

It was with these thoughts in mind that we began to incorporate peer learning into the teaching programme as a way of giving MBA students some insight into the nature of relationships and influence in teams and organizations. Our thinking was guided by the need to have the programme resonate with the organization theory material that students meet in their course, particularly the emerging literature on alternatives to traditional bureaucratic and authoritarian control models.

Aims of team-based learning

Our adoption of peer learning practices had a quite diverse set of aims. They were:

- to produce business graduates who have basic skills for working in and leading teams;
- to provide a learning environment in which students can explore theories and skills for team management and develop, through discovery, their own creative and innovative strategies for achieving team effectiveness;
- to offer students an activity through which they can explore the development of skills associated with reflective learning, and thus
- to prepare students for advanced self-development and experientially based management skill learning programmes;
- to help students discover ways of achieving coordination in organizations – other than through authority, compliance and obedience – by exploring the effects of relationships on behaviour;
- to create a learning environment in which students' enquiry and reflection is informed by consideration of changing organizational forms.

Design and implementation

The choice of the particular form of peer learning was largely determined by our desire to give all students (and not merely those who later select to major in management) a taste of two things: to prepare them for future management roles – the experience of intentional skill development and an acquaintance with reflective learning as described by Brockbank and McGill (1998). Thus, of the many distinguishable forms of peer learning, we chose collaborative group work as the most appropriate form. The programme's emphasis on group interaction and reflection was designed to produce learning outcomes that cannot be attained through tutor-driven experiential activity nor through forms of flexible learning such as computer-mediated learning.

The choice of topic and task area for peer learning activity is similarly guided by the broad expectations we have for peer learning. We have noted informally over several years that students often find group work difficult, unrewarding and frustrating. Teachers in many subjects use group projects because they think it likely that students will somehow automatically learn from each other and that group working and group learning is unquestionably a good thing. In reality, in many courses, the tutor's knowledge of group dynamics is minimal and the nature of the decision to include a group project in the semester's work programme can be more a case of hoping for the right outcome than planning for the conditions that give rise to group effectiveness. Thus the announcement of the group project at the beginning of the semester will often trigger a flurry of manoeuvring by students to get into a 'good' group – one that they think will work well and has the sort of membership with which they feel comfortable. In the culturally diverse classroom the locals often try to avoid working with international students whose level of English speaking and writing may be perceived as not up to standard. The 'ghettoization' of the classroom becomes complete when the various ethnic groups coalesce for reasons of mutual support and communication comfort. By the time students reach their final year, their accumulation of either narrow or negative group project experiences can be substantial – at a time when they are undertaking perhaps the most difficult group project of all – a business strategy simulation.

The skills to be learned

We send a clear signal to students that this is not just another group project by referring to it as a 'management skills practicum', or 'skills prac', which uses peer learning as its skill-development vehicle. Most of the topics in our subject have obvious theory and skill components. Rather than choose topics such as job design, conflict, negotiation or decision making as the target for peer learning, the most synergy arguably comes from having peer learning groups carrying out writing projects on group dynamics while at the same time studying and analysing the dynamics of their own team. This approach exposes students to key aspects of group leadership from both an experiential and a theoretical point of view. It is designed to help them understand the basic properties of groups, appreciate the development stages that groups go through, see groups as problematical but likely to respond to skilled facilitation, struggle to experiment with developing their own facilitation skills and experience reflection as a way of linking experience with theory.

Elements of the peer learning programme

The role of the tutor

Tutors are asked to use a method whereby students are systematically allocated to peer learning groups and not permitted to self-select. Many groups thus start life with several potentially differentiating features – cultural, language and gender diversity. Students are advised that this procedure is a reflection of what can happen with group formation in business environments.

Peer learning group meetings are programmed to take place in the last hour of the weekly three-hour class meeting. Most groups are able to hold 10 meetings over a 14-week semester. Some hold extra meetings outside class hours and others hold fewer because of absenteeism. The job of the tutor is to facilitate the early development of the group and gradually withdraw to a consultant role as the groups become more confident. Tutors are specifically asked to resist attempts by groups to enrol them as arbitrators, problem solvers or *de facto* leaders. The key skill they thus model is feedback. If a group is having process or task problems, the tutor's assistance is limited to observing group process and feeding back to the group. The tutor's script for dealing with frustrated groups and individuals is to suggest that the activity is a skill-exploration programme, that if the group is having problems then this constitutes a rich learning opportunity and that strategies for dealing with process problems can be found in the literature the group is gathering for its task. Advice is mostly limited to reminding students of the literature resources they have at their disposal, encouraging them to regularly review group process norms and encouraging norms of openness and trust.

The resource booklet

Students are issued with a booklet providing the briefing for the team task. It also includes an overall rationale, expected learning outcomes, learning journal requirements, formatted pages for weekly journal entries, ice breakers and exercises for the early meetings, team climate assessment questionnaire, advice on conducting productive meetings, a briefing for conducting a final meeting, illustrative excerpts from previous learning journals and an article on group facilitation skills.

The reflective learning journal

People are all reflective to varying extents but not necessarily in an effective, learning way. Brown, Bull and Pendlebury (1997: 47) suggest that reflective practice assignments 'measure capacity to analyse and evaluate experience in the light of theories and research evidence'. This is broadly what we mean to achieve by requiring students to keep an individual learning journal. The ability to reflect in a purposeful, theory-informed, structured way on critical group incidents and on one's own actions should arguably prove useful in the business career of the future where individual and organizational learning will be emphasized. Regular entries in the learning journal aim to force the focus of reflection on to the self and personal action using a framework of theory. We expect students to get progressively better throughout the semester at using theory to interpret their own and the group's behaviour. Learning journals are assessed in these terms and the allocation of a substantial percentage of marks for journal writing provides an incentive – especially for those students who find reflection a chore.

The group task

The task for each group is to produce a substantial written report on a nominated aspect of group dynamics. The set task is the same for all groups. Here is an example of a task briefing:

> The task for your skills prac team is to write a *guide book* for use by members of student project teams, to help the teams to function more effectively.

There are many occasions when students engage in group-based work. Some examples would be: project teams working cooperatively on a piece of research and writing; groups forming in the classroom to engage in learning simulations; teams which meet outside the classroom to compete in a strategy game; formal and informal study groups. These situations constitute rich learning opportunities which can establish the skills necessary for the many group experiences that your career will offer – experiences such as participating in joint client/consultant project team management, leading a project team, being a member of a self-managing work team, facilitating more productive team meetings. The learning benefits of student group work will be harvested more readily if group members have a framework for examining groups and a map of the skills that help us lead groups. Your team task is to create the framework and the map.

Your Guide Book must address the following issues:

> What are group process factors and why are they important?
> What factors determine the effective operation of groups?
> What skills are appropriate for leading groups?
> What are facilitation skills and how can a group be lead in a facilitative way?

The end product should be a document which could be handed to the members of a student project group and which would provide guidance on what problems to expect in a small group and how to confront those problems, what behaviours are characteristic of good group members and how to lead a group facilitatively.

As you carry out the work for this paper, you should, from Day 1, observe the development of your own skills prac group and attempt to apply the ideas you are researching to your group. For example, if you are reading about team-building techniques, you should try some of them out in your group. If you are reading about team leader behaviour, try out the material in your group. As you come to understand what behaviours promote group openness and communication flow, deliberately practise those behaviours and discuss the effects on your group climate. Remember, your joint assignment and your individual reflective journal will be assessed not only on academic content but also on evidence of your growing awareness of what is happening psychologically in the group. You must continually be using what you are reading theoretically to expand your understanding of what is happening experientially. Thus, you will be acquiring the skills of group facilitation.

Evaluating the peer learning programme

We requested students to make available copies of their individual learning journals and team project reports, in confidence, for research purposes. Most obliged willingly. We also administered an end-of-semester project evaluation questionnaire.

Survey data

One hundred and fifty students from the same semester cohort completed the evaluation questionnaire. The mean age was thirty-one and the range from twenty to forty-eight. The cohort had an average of nine years work experience and 3.4 years management experience. Sixty per cent of the sample was male.

Students reported broad satisfaction with their peer learning experience. They saw the programme as worthwhile, challenging and yielding some useful skills. They found it a challenge to write the reflective journal but most saw it as an effective learning device.

We cross-tabulated all the attitude items in the questionnaire with age, years of work experience, years of management experience, gender and cultural background. No significant relationships were noted. Students' survey evaluations of peer learning do not appear to depend on these variables.

Analysis of learning journals

The individual journals were collated into their respective groups. Group journals were analysed until dominant patterns began to form in the data. Discourse analysis (Fairclough, 1992, 1995; and Van Dijk, 1997) was applied within a grounded theory framework developed from the work of Eisenhardt (1989) and Strauss and Corbin (1990). This analysis involved the assessment of each paragraph of text within each sampled journal for an underlying theme. The theme was recorded as a one-word concept. We then compared the relationship between thematic and demographic data across individual journals and across groups in order to identify patterns. This process was continued until emerging patterns saturated.

The dominant demographic factors that emerged were language skills, international or local student, gender, work experience and age. The dominant thematic concepts that emerged were power and differentiation together with diversity, relationship and function.

Power and differentiation

By power and differentiation we mean the basis by which students see themselves as different from other members of their group with respect to their perceived level of influence. Language is a prominent differentiating factor as is culture, gender and work experience. In many instances the groups broke into local and international subgroups where the local students appeared, almost unwittingly, to adopt the superior role, dominating and directing international students. Within their journals many local students discussed their frustration with the international students' seeming unwillingness to take an active role in the group's activities. A journal excerpt illustrates this:

> These international students' unwillingness to participate is profound, which can be attributed to their cultural respect for authority and generally anyone older. . . I am somewhat displeased with my inability to motivate these guys into greater participation and pro-active decision making. . . the cultural differences coupled with moderate intellectual abilities (apart from X who appears to be the smartest of the group, yet, ironically, the most withdrawn) are hurdles too great to be overcome by sheer will and design alone.

In contrast, international students, a high proportion of whom had English as a second language, saw themselves in a somewhat subordinate position and were therefore reluctant to take their 'voice' in the group. They wrote about how their language difficulties left them feeling inadequate, how their cultural conditioning made it difficult for them to make sense of the project as well as their group members' behaviour and their fear of losing face in such circumstances. The underlying theme that pervaded these students' journal reflections was: 'the contribution I can make is limited and I am worried that I may be perceived as inferior.' The result was the creation of boundaries of identity that reflected an 'us' and 'them' theme. An extract from one international student's journal shows this:

> I felt excluded because the communication flew among those active speakers who have English as mother tongue and other members who do not have English as a mother tongue chose to keep our ideas inside because we are not trusting other members and we were afraid that we may be laughed or looked down on by others. . . the Western style of teaching (which I think is used by Australia) guarantees the student to speak freely. . . I tried to participate in the discussion, I appreciate that the native speaker sub group were willing to listen to our broken English. I started to build up my trust to the group.

Accordingly, mixed groups tended to be dominated by native English speaker(s) who seemed almost compelled to take charge. The discourse of these students appeared to demonstrate an assumed superiority underpinned by a belief that they were more able than the other members of their group. The underlying theme was: 'I am burdened by these less capable group members with respect to this task.' These students were very much focused upon themselves and what the other members could do or not do for them in regard to achieving their desired marks and grades.

Rarely did local students reflect other than superficially on the cultural and language factors limiting international students' participation in group leadership and decision making. Some reported feeling uncomfortable with their uncontested position of dominance but were prepared to live with it in order to get the task completed. In a number of groups, the frustratingly low contribution of international students was explained away as laziness and a lack of commitment to the team.

We had hoped that students would come to see culturally mixed groups as an example of the sort of challenging team performance problems that occur in the business world where, for example, systems analysts and programmers have to work with marketing managers and accountants, who are faced with overcoming 'language' problems associated with a lack of understanding of each other's disciplines, perspectives and interests. This level of insight happened rarely. As locals came to realize that they were in positions of uncontested dominance, they appeared to accept this as the natural order of things, and drove the group towards task completion. In consequence open conflict was often avoided and opportunities to explore diversity were bypassed.

Diversity

In the initial stages of group activity both local and international students expressed their concern that the diverse cultural and ideological perspectives in the group might have a negative effect on group functioning. They discussed their frustration at making collective sense of what needed to be done and how it was going to be achieved. However as the members developed shared understanding of the group task – what Weick (1995) would refer to as 'consensual sense codes' – their concerns with diversity were alleviated and they became more capable of working and functioning together. Groups that did not develop consensus continued to find it difficult to deal with diversity.

Relationship

Similarly, those groups – particularly culturally mixed groups – in which members developed a set of mutually rewarding relationships, exhibited a cohesiveness that members valued and that gave them, individually and collectively, a real voice. In those groups which did not develop cohesively, members tended to express concern about the boundaries of differentiation and about how other group members were undermining their performance.

Function

Some students wrote of a need for structure, direction and leadership. For these members, the group appeared to be lost and going nowhere with respect to pursuit of goals. In most cases other members of the group did not have the same concern. This was not a cultural phenomenon, rather it appeared to be linked to the students' functional background. For instance many of those who expressed concern were from engineering or accounting professions.

Discussion

A major aim of our peer learning programme was to have students learn to deal with group process problems – to learn basic facilitation skills experientially. We hoped that some – ideally all – students would move out from the safe familiarity of passive cognitive learning to take on the risks of experiential learning where the challenge lies in dealing with the emotional implications of one's place in a social system. For a number of groups this indeed happened. One or more members of the group were able to experiment successfully with facilitation skills. They variously modelled and promoted open communication, promoted trust building, took risks, asked for and gave feedback, challenged negative norms and helped deal with conflict in an open and mature way. For a number of groups and individuals, however, the cultural and linguistic barriers prevented them from seeing even the possibility of experimenting with group process. Once influence patterns in the group began to gel in favour of a cultural/linguistic subgroup, all experimenting seemed to stop, process norms went unchallenged, and although the task was completed – in many cases to a high standard – the ideal of shared leadership and true collaborative learning was not achieved. Where differentiated groups did achieve high-quality task output there was almost always a driving individual or subgroup that did much of the work on behalf of the disempowered students.

The outcomes of our peer learning programme were, therefore, in part, a product of the context in which they are conducted. The aims of peer learning can be compromised by process problems such as social differentiation occurring within the learning group. These problems are not always visible in the classroom nor in the final group written report. The keeping of reflective journals however, opened a window through which we could view social differentiation. Reflective writing revealed many of the contextual factors that allowed local students, particularly those with a high level of work experience, to dominate groups. This came about mainly because international students appeared to disempower themselves by doubting their ability to make a contribution to the group. They were aided and abetted in this by the willingness of local students to occupy the leadership roles de facto. It appeared to be an unintended yet mutual relationship in which one party is privileged and the other is marginalized. The result however, is that both parties become frustrated with each other, in some cases to the point of total inability to function as a group.

It is important for MBA students to consider how forms of differentiation come about because contemporary management thinking promotes the use of empowerment, which represents the de-differentiation of power relationships (Clegg, 1990) and a shift to consensual decision making and concertive control (Barker, 1993). Such a shift requires group members to focus on the maintenance of each participant's 'voice'. Students recognized the forms of differentiation occurring within their groups and discussed how it affected them, but they stopped short at considering why it occurred. This has clear implications for the design of peer learning programmes in a people management course. Incentives need to be built into the peer learning programme to motivate participants to risk confronting the problem of differentiation. To explore this issue further, we interviewed a number of students and discussed our findings with them. This revealed a further dimension that affected our peer learning programme – one stemming from the students' broader needs and expectations within the MBA programme.

Students argued that 'they are not an endless resource', that our subject was only one of a number they were studying and they could allocate only a certain amount of time to assessment activities. Thus, for many students and in particular local students, there is pressure to focus on 'only what I have to do' to get the desired result. The exertions of experiential learning are not automatically seen as appealing and leading to useful skill development.

Furthermore, the MBA is an expensive undertaking. Many students cannot afford to lose marks let alone fail because of the poor performance of other members of their team. A number of students strongly voiced their disappointment with having to coach those with poor English. Similarly, many students with a high level of work experience found it frustrating to work with students who had only minimal work experience because the latter were perceived as being unable to contribute equally. Another point of friction was with high-achieving students who were seeking distinction grades having to work in the same group with students content with a mere pass.

These issues complicate the design of our peer learning programme and highlight the role that assessment plays in programme design. Linking assessment to programme aims is fundamental for educators. What we have learned from this project however, is that without exploring this link at a deeper level, in our case through the analysis of students' journals, educators may not know if the aims of their programme are being undermined by contextual variables. We may have to change the focus of our assessment in order to encourage students to confront the sorts of group divisions we have described.

Conclusions

Many students just do not understand the idea of group facilitation – of seeing groups as essentially problematical and using a set of social skills to explore and solve process problems. If we examine payoffs for disturbing versus maintaining group harmony it may be that to address process and performance problems would be a major risk and an uncomfortable experience for group members even though they are aware of the theory and practice of group facilitation. The payoff would be uncertain because the time frame of one semester might not permit a quantum improvement in the team output (the report), or because of a perceived lack of skill, high risk of failure and conflict. We have to accept also that some students have little desire to explore intercultural differences. For these reasons, our invitation to students to use peer learning to develop and practise group facilitation skills was not always taken up the way we intended.

This is not to suggest that the inactivated facilitation role necessarily means lack of insight into group process. Implicit learning can still take place while explicit behavioural exploration is being suppressed. The payoff for risky intervention in and confrontation of group processes may simply not be high enough for many students. Real-world business pressures can undoubtedly provide sufficiently compelling reasons for risking facilitative interventions as many managers have discovered when faced with leading a low-performing team. We cannot hope to simulate the intensity and realism of such reasons in the classroom but we can attempt to convince the student that experiential peer learning is an appropriate way to learn people management skills.

We have begun to address some of the issues outlined above. Specifically, we are:

- redesigning our assessment criteria to focus student attention on the exploration and management of social differentiation;
- making our expectations about cooperative group learning more explicit in the briefing materials we give to students;
- alerting students to problems of intercultural communication and helping groups move these problems into the realm of the discussable;
- reweighting the importance of the reflective journal and handing out resource material to help with crosscultural communications;
- promoting the argument that the group learning experience is a worthwhile form of learning because it amounts to a microcosm of the social diversity found in the business world;
- reassuring students that although they may not possess sufficiently developed interpersonal communication skills to gain maximum benefit from team-based learning, there is much to be gained from *some* experimentation and *some* reflection;
- searching for ways to assist all students to appreciate the learning utility of regular, written reflection.

Our experience with peer learning has taught us to look for the hidden barriers that the learning context may put between the educator's objectives and the peer learning outcomes that the students actually achieve. The next step in our peer learning programme is to develop ways of helping learners remove the barriers.

References

Barker, J (1993) Tightening the iron cage: concertive control in self managed teams, *Administrative Science Quarterly*, **38**, pp 408–37

Beck, J (1994) The new paradigm of management education, *Management Learning*, **25** (2), pp 231–47

Boud, D (ed) (1988) *Developing Student Autonomy in Learning,* Kogan Page, London

Brockbank, A and McGill, I (1998) *Facilitating Reflective Learning in Higher Education,* SRHE and Open University Press, Buckingham

Brown, G, Bull, J and Pendlebury, M (1997) *Assessing Student Learning in Higher Education,* Routledge, London

Clegg, S (1990) *Modern Organizations: Organization studies for the postmodern world,* Sage, London

Clegg, S and Hardy, C (1996) Some dare call it power, in *Handbook of Organization Studies* (eds) S Clegg, C Hardy and W Nord, Sage, London

Eisenhardt, K (1989) Building theory from case study research, *Academy of Management Review*, **14** (4), pp 532–50

Fairclough, N (1992) *Discourse and Social Change*, Polity Press, Cambridge

Fairclough, N (1995) *Critical Discourse Analysis*, Longman, London

Porter, L and McKibbin, L (1988) *Management Education and Development: Drift or thrust into the 21st Century,* McGraw-Hill, New York

Rynes, S and Trank, C (1999) Behavioral science in the business school curriculum: teaching in a changing institutional environment, *Academy of Management Review*, **24** (4), pp 808–24

Strauss, A and Corbin, J (1990) *Basics of Qualitative Research: Grounded theory procedures and techniques,* Sage, Newbury Park CA

Van Dijk, T (1997) The study of discourse, in *Discourse as Structure and Process* (ed) Van Dijk T, Sage, London

Weick, K (1995) *Sensemaking in Organizations*, Sage, London

7

Project management teams: a model of best practice in design

Jenny Toynbee Wilson

A problem is identified

My decision to introduce peer learning was prompted by an increase from 60 to 90 students with no budget for additional academic and technical staff. This caused an immediate dilemma: how to manage the demands of novice undergraduate students undertaking a holistic curriculum organized around project-based, experiential learning and reflective practice in the first year, second semester core subject 'visual communication' in a design degree.

The strategy of teaching and learning in the design studio is exemplified by Donald Schön (1987) who describes it as 'reflection-in-action'. Schön presents a scenario of constant interaction between teacher and learner in a one-to-one relationship that relies on offering frequent informal feedback on work in progress. This master/apprentice approach, which epitomizes the traditional teaching/learning strategy in design, engages both teacher and learner in an ongoing dialogue of 'show and tell' using drawings to explain the process of visual thinking and to illustrate how a concept may be developed.

First-year students, even in a class of 90, are expected to optimize their creativity and produce individual responses to assessment tasks undertaken as design projects. Students produce a 'package' of components providing evidence of learning, which is assessed according to a range of criteria. A typical 'package' consists of the design of a visual communication project presented with a written and oral rationale, a portfolio containing annotated visuals indicating the design process, a research document; interview surveys, user tests and analysis and a reflective diary.

With what had become a staff/student ratio of 1:45 it was clearly impossible to offer individual attention each week to every student. To supervise the processing of projects and the criteria-based assessment of 90 individual design projects effectively appeared as an insurmountable problem. I could no longer rely on traditional strategies. The time had come to rethink my practice and make some radical change.

Instant solution

Group work seemed to be an obvious solution and consistent with our teaching/learning strategies modelled on professional design practice, which relies heavily on group participation and teamwork. Designers expect to elicit from and offer ongoing feedback to colleagues as they progress a project from initial concept to final realization. As all visualized concepts must be produced with the assistance of specialists through complex media technologies such as print, video and digital interactives, teamwork is essential. Although the establishment of design teams to work on joint projects is a major feature of design study in later years, group work had not been at all successful in the first semester of the first year. In fact the results of subject evaluation had been so negative that group work had been abandoned.

Previous experience of group work

The subject of group work had been introduced in a focus group. Students' comments were a reaction to the overall management and assessment of the project. Each student in a group had received the same assessment mark regardless of individual performance or group involvement. Students, attempting to establish themselves in a new learning environment, complained bitterly about the uneven workload, the lack of specific skills by some group members, and the non-involvement of others, which had left them with a sense of inequity, unfairness and considerable discontent.

I could understand why reaction to group work was so negative. Entry to the course is highly competitive. For the majority it is based on an aggregate mark achieved in high school exams. Students therefore enrol in design with very different levels of understanding, visual literacy, technical skills and motivation. Management of the course had not been sensitive to the competitive nature of novice students. Moreover, at this early stage, students must gain an understanding of very unfamiliar content, experience unaccustomed methods of teaching and learning and acquire many new skills and competencies. As a consequence, individual performance is very erratic as few students have the necessary experience to discriminate and assess the relative merit of their work at any stage and therefore what each can offer and receive of value in the context of group work.

Finding a solution

A solution had to answer the first problem of how to handle the complex demands of the increased number of novice students attempting to study in a way that was foreign to them and dilute the negative effect of over-competitive behaviour. The second problem was how to reduce the incremental increase in time spent on formative and ultimately summative assessment. It was essential to maintain the model of design practice and the important characteristics of experiential learning that developed each student's ability to engage in an unfamiliar process of reflective action to learn how to visually refine their budding ideas. It became evident that I had to rethink my practice and find a way of enriching rather than diminishing the learning experience.

The self-directed learner

Ultimately, the problem became one of how to change comfortable habits; how to be flexible and innovative. In particular, how to accept the risk and emotional upset of failure so easily expressed in the anger and disappointment of students' comments when the time came for subject evaluation. I reread some texts for support and inspiration. The answer came from Malcolm Knowles (1975) who reminded me that: 'creative leaders make a different set of assumptions (essentially positive) about human nature from the assumptions (essentially negative) made by controlling leaders'. Knowles claims that the highest function of leadership is 'releasing the energy of the people in the system and managing the process for giving that energy direction towards mutually beneficial goals'. John Dewey (1933) reinforced this when describing the methodology of education for professional practice: 'initiation into the tradition is the means by which the powers of learners are released and directed'. Paul Ramsden (1991) put these statements into context: 'effective university teaching includes a commitment to encouraging student independence which requires active learning through responsible cooperative endeavour'.

Realigning perceptions

My reading refreshed my resolve to counteract the damaging effect of competitive methods and stimulate the positive effect of cooperative learning. The only solution to the problem lay in realigning my perceptions – in short I had to relinquish my need to control the teaching and learning situation and see the students not as a burden but as a valuable resource.

Convincing the students

Group work was the only answer but it had to be planned creatively to counteract a recent bad experience. Above all, group work had to be managed sensitively to ensure the learning experience would be positive. It had to be introduced in a way that would sufficiently convince students that group work was both an essential and beneficial aspect of professional design practice so that it would be acknowledged as valid and potentially valuable. The value to students of involving them in a cooperative process of critical enquiry and reflection leading to improved judgement and ultimately the ability to self and peer assess, was promoted by indicating how designers rely on constant feedback from peers to optimize concepts and manage the production process. This led to the conclusion that designers must develop good interpersonal communication skills and be prepared to value innovation but be analytically critical of personal ideas in the light of experienced collective opinion.

Of equal importance was to present the 'win/win' opportunity offered through collaboration in gathering research, resource information, technical knowledge and skill sharing. Finally, I had to indicate how individual effort could be minimized by collective planning and decision making that would assist individual project management through the group's responsibility to help members maintain time schedules and critical deadlines.

By initiating cooperative learning through responsible group behaviour I hoped that competition would be reduced and that any positive experience gained through the mutual support of a group would influence future learning experiences. My underlying aims were to foster a greater sense of self-confidence, self-reliance and understanding between students from different cultures, ages and sexes and assist the process of orientation to university culture and group socialisation.

Introduction of project management groups

The peer learning groups were initially, and continue to be introduced with a professional seminar introducing a number of design case studies emphasizing the value of informal feedback from peers, the need for team work to process and complete a project and the critical nature of good project management. It is explained that although each student is to produce an individual project, specific components will be undertaken through group work and peer assessed. The design practice model and the topic of project management are reiterated before establishing the project management groups. The reflective comments from students in previous years have become a valuable and convincing aid. A selection of opinions, both good and bad, is used on overheads to focus on specific issues. Feedback from each year is collated in easily accessible folders.

The process

Whenever possible, each group is self-selected and comprises no less than three, or more than five students. Each student receives a project brief, which requires the design and final presentation of a prototype for a 'new deck of playing cards' based on the research and personal interpretation of the four alchemaic elements of fire, earth, water and ether (air). The project involves students initially in the research and development of alternative image, symbol, numeric and hierarchical systems of visual communication. The first prototype must be tested on potential users for engagement, understanding and functionality before finally being refined for presentation. The briefing documents also include an outline project time line, a page of 'helpful hints' for project management and group work, notes on initiating a user testing survey and a blank assessment form indicating the project components to be submitted and assessment criteria. More recently I have added a 'trouble-shooter' form that students can use collectively or individually when a problem arises.

Once settled into a group, each is asked to choose a group name and discuss the five most essential criteria for positive group work with the aim of establishing expectations of one another through consensus. This information is submitted the next week having been entered into a pro forma as peer assessment on group work. Thereafter, during scheduled class time, the Project Management Groups are expected to meet and discuss work in progress according to a time schedule mutually devised and agreed upon. There is considerable evidence that many groups meet regularly at other times. Most favoured locations are in the library to share research tasks, in the computer labs to help one another with report writing and project processing and in the coffee shop for a break.

Monitoring the process

The inclusion of a 'troubleshooter' form has been helpful in indicating to students that problems may occur with which they will have to deal collectively or individually. The form consists of an A5 page that contains the heading, space for the group's name and members taking responsibility for writing the form and also the student/s who are to receive it. I have known groups to use the 'troubleshooter' to assert themselves by suggesting to a member seen as an 'autocratic bully. . . to cool it and listen for a change'. Students are encouraged to see the 'troubleshooter' as a last resort and, before sending, it must be countersigned by my teaching partner or myself. The troubleshooter can be used by individuals to alert me to intervene when difficulties occur that cannot be handled collectively or personally. This happens rarely but cases of bullying, sexism and racism have created tensions requiring sensitive handling and ongoing monitoring. In all situations advance warning helps to minimize and often solve problems before they become compounded.

Student feedback from a randomly selected group

Over the last five years I have adapted and refined the strategy as student evaluation and feedback suggests areas of improvement and this will continue. Still at issue is whether peer learning groups should be random, socially engineered or self-selected. In my experience, randomly selected groups even out the strengths and weaknesses of individual students but create problems of inequitable responsibility and frustration which are felt by the more involved students who feel they are carrying the 'no hopers' and 'freeloaders'.

The following feedback from five students in the same randomly selected group indicates that the experience may not be commonly shared with each student having a very different perspective:

I felt that only half of us were seriously interested in work, the others just socialized and drank coffee – great for them but tough on us who were keen. [Amanda 1997]

From a similarly disgruntled student:

since I had a computer at home I seemed to get stuck doing all the report writing. [Glen 1997]

Another aspect of this situation is revealed in this remark:

I felt left out because the others were so much better because they had money and a computer at home so I didn't know what I could do. [Teresa 1997]

Two from the same group stated more positively:

I really enjoyed the experience of sharing my computer skills and even although I was loaded with work I was happy to let them buy me coffee instead. [Rob 1997]

It was such a help having the group to help me work on the computer . . . I learned so much and tried to do my bit by being patient with the silly stuff and listening. [Kate 1997]

Self-selected groups

Socially engineering the groups seems the only way possible to ensure a mix of sexes, ages and cultures. Although the assimilation of minority groups remains an aim, students are suspicious of the motives and less willing to participate if they feel they are being used to solve a problem that is not of their making. So I have resisted this method in favour of quiet persuasion for self-selected groups to be more inclusive. Since the introductory year when random groups were established by drawing from a hat, groups have self-selected, which was the system voted for by over 90 per cent of the students the following year. Such groups are certainly most effective for the well-motivated students who invariably choose to work with others of the same inclination. Feedback from these groups is always most favourable and a constant affirmation that the strategy is valuable.

Student feedback from self-selected groups

Over the five years of implementing peer learning, student feedback makes it abundantly clear that students gain much from the experience. Although favourable responses came from over 75 per cent of the total group in 1998 a selection chosen to indicate the spectrum received follows. A typical favourable comment is:

> This was the most enjoyable group project ever. . . being given a different perspective on your work helps you to improve. . . I thoroughly recommend this kind of group work. . . not only do you meet more people, you similarly advance your own designs. [Yvette 1998]

From a male student persuaded to join a group of females:

> I've never worked with girls before. . . it was amazing. . . they were so organized and helpful. . . I sincerely enjoyed the process. . . and the lollies brought to class sure helped my creative genius. [Michael 1998]

Improved project management

Another student mentions the value of project management:

> The team performance was rewarding with group brainstorming giving us the encouragement to explore concepts that appealed. Meeting in class meant there was little inconvenience and used our time well. Constant weekly feedback certainly helped improve our designs. With the combination of the best skills of one person meshed with the talents of another, better than expected results were achieved. Continual reporting indicated a good level of communication and also how communication advances personal relationships between our peers. [Ada 1998]

Some important insights came to an older mature female student:

> Working in the group was a very useful experience. Being much older, group members tended to ask me for feedback, so I soon learned I had to ask for more myself. . . the honest feedback and synergy especially at the concept stages saved many hours of tearing down fruitless paths and led to a much higher evolution of the design process than working as individuals would have achieved. [Annette 1998]

Morale and motivation

A number of comments refer to the motivation stimulated by group work:

> The morale factor was something I had not counted on gaining. . . it was a boost having the support of others to give encouragement and keep you working apace with them. . . we gradually developed a really good rapport and 'team' feel which was good for me because I am usually a very independent operator and came to the exercise with rather a negative attitude towards the whole 'group' thing but I feel I have totally overcome this so it was a very positive experience because I learned a lot about how a group can strengthen personal resolve rather than inhibit it. [Emma 1998]

Communication

Although counterproductive to an aim of assimilation, students from similar cultures and backgrounds also prefer self-selected groups. Feedback from students forming groups differentiated by language indicate the positive aspects for them:

> We like to show respect for each other which is not common with Australian students. [Chun Lu 1998]

> It is sometimes such a relief to be able to work together with others that speak Mandarin because we can really communicate well and feel happy together having a good time for a change. [Cindy 1998]

> This was so good. . . I was not on my own feeling fearful of not understanding. [Tin Lan 1998]

When reluctant to mix, communication can be seriously hampered by language differences:

> This has been hell because of problems with language. . .never again. [Anthony 1998]

> Half the time I didn't understand what was going on because only some of us spoke English. . .the others I haven't a clue. [Sam 1998]

Cultural norms can also create upset:

> the group was so meek, no one person would initiate anything so I felt I always had to. [Sanjeev 1998]

> I am always polite and obedient in class. . .I have not been taught to argue loudly about my ideas. [Jay 1998]

Often unexpected outcomes are discovered:

> This experience was so useful in deciphering the project brief. Together we discussed all the complications of the project and as I usually ignore the instructions to get things done quicker . . . this made me confront them. The group wouldn't let me get away with being slack so my project finished up better than usual. [Ben 1998]

> The discussion each week really helped. I started to really understand the brief, what was meant. . . what was required. . . what was expected. . .we double checked the details and made sure we knew what to present. [Mary 1998]

Time management

Time and project management is often the subject of feedback:

> For the first time ever I hit the deadline. I definitely have to work on my time management in future. In the group I was forced to keep up each week as agreed in our schedule otherwise I would have procrastinated because I cannot make a decision and stick to it. When I stuffed around the group jumped on me and gave me no chance to change my mind. [Victoria 1998]

A similar comment comes from another student:

> My time management improved so well by working in the group because I did not want to let them down. I learned a lot from this. . . how to stick to a time line and work schedule to keep on top of the workload. [Lucette 1998]

Problems with self-selected groups

However, peer learning groups can also polarize into extremes that occur more often when groups self-select. The problems encountered when poorly motivated or weak students work together can be very difficult to manage. The work produced for assessment is often well below the standard achieved by each individual. Self-selected groups can be a disastrous experience for well-motivated students who finish up in 'left over' groups with members of a different inclination.

Group dynamics being what they are, issues are compounded, energy levels diminish exponentially and the anger and resentment that can develop between ill-matched members can be incredibly distressing and damaging to interest and motivation. This negative learning experience can be difficult to turn around unless detected early enough to mediate. Typical comments from students refer to the frustration caused by absent and uncommitted members:

> It was difficult to work in a group when not everyone was there at the same time. [Gideon 1998]

> I wasted so much time waiting around for the group to turn up in class. [Jane 1998]

> This was just an awful experience. . . the boys were so rude and just joked and made destructive comments all the time. . . then they left me with all the work and went to the pub. [Janet 1998]

> As far as I'm concerned. . . working with a group just sucks! [Christopher 1998]

The 'troubleshooter' has helped to minimize such problems and these comments present a minority opinion, but problems of incompatibility continue to occur particularly as those first year students who have decided to withdraw at the end of the semester lack the motivation to be involved.

Regardless of briefings, written 'helpful hints' on group work and occasional damage control, a few students indicate their lack of understanding the aims of group work and report on their disinterest and non-involvement:

> I just got on with my own project and didn't bother turning up. [Robert 1998]

The most negative remarks come from students who appear to have gained nothing from the experience other than instant outrage:

> What a futile exercise. . . I could not see the point of it. . . I wasn't interested in their work or what they had to say. . . what do they know. . . who needs a group anyway? [Sean 1998]

Although claiming considerable discontent this student, on reflection, gained some essential realization:

> I did not understand why we should work together since we were not doing a group project and being assessed on it. I hate group projects anyway. . . please never again. . . if this is what it's like then maybe design is not for me. [Annie 1998]

Sometimes the comments are an honest admission of self-interest to the detriment of peer learning:

> I did not work well as part of the group. I found it difficult to interact with the others because I was so tied up with my own project and worried about my design that it was hard to give anyone else any time or energy. However I know I must get used to this as being a designer means working with others. It may take a bit of time but I have definitely learned from this experience. [Caroline 1998]

Improved understanding

In summary, feedback is very varied in terms of what each student perceives as important. By far the majority conclude that their learning experience has been enriched:

> My eyes have been opened. [Michael 1998]

> Through collaboration the project became a dynamic learning experience. [Tiffany 1998]

An invaluable mechanism for process motivation which brought a great deal of understanding and insight into how we operate creatively as individuals and as a group. [Julie 1998]

We found this project engaging and enjoyable and group work really beneficial as we learned so much from one another. I can't wait to continue this next year. [Heather 1998]

Assessment of peer learning

One of the primary motives for initiating group work was to engage students in the process of critically analysing the work of others to offer continuous feedback as individual projects progressed. A further aim was to start the shift from a teacher focus to independent learning by encouraging peer assessment, which would then enable students to reflect more objectively on their own work and develop the skills and confidence to assess themselves more effectively and accurately. There is considerable literature on the value, validity and reliability of peer assessment (Falchikov, 2001). Simplistically, it is the process of students marking the work of other students. In practice, students must agree to act responsibly in giving and receiving assessment. This was gradually introduced and practised over the weeks leading to final project submission as the student groups became more willing and able to offer one another informal feedback.

In the first week students had received a copy of the project components and assessment criteria which had been discussed in order to explain the learning objectives and indicate those to be peer assessed. Over the five weeks of the project, to help focus on relevant and valuable feedback, the groups were encouraged to refer to the learning objectives and discuss how learning had to be in evidence through the project submission and what criteria were used for assessment. By the deadline most students seemed to be clear of expectations and confident to undertake the task. Basically each Project Management Group assessed the work of students from another group.

Peer assessment of project work

The stages of the peer assessment process were as follows:

1. We recapped the meaning of each criterion and where evidence should be found.

2.   Additional assessment documents were distributed to each student with a SWOP (Strengths, Weaknesses and Opportunities for improvement) sheet for note taking.
3.   Each student completed personal details and attached the SWOP sheet to their project work.
4.   Student groups rotated the work being assessed to enable each student to individually examine the work, take notes and write explanatory comments on the SWOP sheet.
5.   Group members shared notes and discussed areas of agreement and differences of opinion.
6.   To ensure equitable standards across all groups, each group then examined the approach and assessment standards made of work by another group.
7.   Groups conferred on the assessment of each student's work for whom they were collectively responsible and completed an assessment form.
8.   Assessment was supplemented by comments culled and consolidated from the explanatory comments written on the SWOP sheet.

Peer assessment of project management groups

Given the commitment and energy required of group involvement and the fact that students judge importance according to assessment value, three of a total of ten assessment criteria related directly to the research, process and project management undertaken through group work. Perhaps of greater value to learning how to improve group work was the feedback given by each student to others in the group. The pro formas listing the five criteria for successful group work originated in the first week were used. These were collected and checked before distribution. When very unfavourable remarks were received they were rewritten on to one feedback page to maintain anonymity and temper as necessary. As the majority claimed to have had a positive experience the feedback reinforced this and brought about a good sense of self-congratulation and closure to the project.

Peer (and later self-) assessment documents were presented with each student's portfolio of work and overviewed by the teaching team of a lecturer and tutor to correlate assessment. Examination of the peer assessment indicated some minor variations between lecturer and peer assessment in a small number of criteria but overall the greatest variation was less than 5 per cent. Each group had taken the responsibility very seriously. Of particular value was the quality of the written feedback, which was accurate, insightful and thoughtfully presented. It offered much more detailed and extensive information than otherwise would have been possible.

Feedback from the student group indicated that, although either sceptical or fearful of the process and reluctant to be critical about the work of their peers, there was general agreement that the process had been a valuable experience and all were positive about undertaking it on other occasions. The group work had provided the collective means to offer objective assessment and also protection from personalized comments. All perceived the peer assessment process as experienced to be fair and equitable. In summary, students acknowledged the importance of having to take responsibility for their opinion and agreed that the mediation of the group had tempered idiosyncratic value judgements. A number stated that it was preferable to teacher assessment because the cross checking, double marking and degree of consensus required had avoided personal values from dominating.

Self-assessment and reflection

After receiving group assessment, each student was asked to study the feedback and assess themselves using the same detailed criteria. Although there was evidence that some students disagreed with their peers, believing their work to be superior, others were self-deprecating and tended to denigrate their achievements.

These issues were able to be discussed at meetings with each group to return work, receive a final reflective statement (personal project management report) and finalize the project. The real value of the total process was conspicuous in the students' reflections on learning. The majority of students indicated that the process had required them to be much more responsible, analytical and reflective. Comments suggested that students were better able to see and articulate:

- what they had done and why;
- what was valued and how they could measure relative success;
- how they could improve performance; and
- how helpful the group work had been in identifying and clarifying the whole process and assessment of design.

Conclusion

Three hours of scheduled contact time were allocated to manage the peer assessment process, which was considerably less than the 20 hours or more spent by each of the teaching team who undertook the parallel assessment. The outcome proved the validity of peer assessment in a supervised environment. The reliability of the results and the feedback from students reinforced my decision to continue and refine the strategy. The benefits of the strategy to the quality of learning also far outweighed concerns to keep all control of assessment in the hands of academic staff who are often reluctant to relinquish any control over their students' learning. Yet this is more a product of tradition and fear of the unknown than any real educational imperative. The evidence of success, which convinced some colleagues to continue the strategy into the next year, was partly because of my enthusiasm and that of my tutor, but mainly a result of reading the student's personal reflections and comments made in the subject evaluation.

As student numbers continue to increase, university teachers will have to become increasingly flexible in the resources they draw on to meet the demands placed on them. Instead of seeing increased student numbers as a problem, the potential of using the students themselves to perform tasks such as peer learning and assessment may offer innovative and valuable solutions. This does not in any way mean that we surrender our responsibilities as teachers. On the contrary, programmes such as this require a coherent structure and direction. It is essential to take the time to plan and develop this structure before involving students, particularly when peer assessment is proposed. Similarly, it takes time and effort to prepare students to both adequately fulfil their roles within the programme and to maximize their own educational benefits from the process. Given this initial investment of time and energy, the benefits can be considerable.

References

Dewey, J (1933) *How We Think: A restatement of reflective thinking to the educative process,* Dover, New York

Falchikov, N (2001) *Learning Together: Peer tutoring in higher education,* Routledge, London

Knowles, M (1975) *Self-Directed Learning: A guide for learners and teachers,* Associated Press, New York

Ramsden, P (1991) *Learning to Teach in Higher Education,* Routledge, London

Schön, D (1987) *Educating the Reflective Practitioner: Toward a new design for teaching and learning in the professions,* Jossey-Bass, San Francisco

8

Peer learning in law: using a group journal

James Cooper

This chapter examines the development of a group journal as a key component of the learning and assessment strategies in business law, a first-year core subject within the Bachelor of Business degree. The development of the journal took place in the context of growing student numbers, continuing budgetary restraints and heavier workloads of lecturers and tutors. This context required a refocusing of the subject to facilitate cooperative learning within groups, and assessment tasks that facilitated critical thinking and learning without increasing the assessment burden of markers.

My aim was to assist in the development of critical thinking and a reflective lifelong learning approach to knowledge amongst students studying business law. I wanted to develop journal writing to encourage students to engage in deeper approaches to learning within a cooperative peer environment. The journal has been modified and changed within the last three years to deal with emerging problems, to introduce more challenging projects to meet the needs of the student groups and to provide more effective assessment mechanisms. Today the use of journals has been accepted as an important mechanism for teaching and learning and is used across a variety of subjects within the Law Faculty.

Context

The subject 'business law' is the introductory law subject in the Bachelor of Business degree and is taken by all first-year students. The subject is offered every semester and was taught originally in the format of one-hour large lectures and a two-hour workshop. With numbers of 500 to 600 students a semester, there were three large lectures and 20 or so workshops employing approximately eight part-time and full-time tutors across two campuses. Due to budgetary and other pressures the subject was reduced from six to four credit points and reformatted to a two-hour large lecture and a one-hour workshop, effectively doubling the load of the remaining tutors. During this period there was a large increase in non-English-speaking background students who faced the daunting task of studying a language and culturally based law subject. As coordinator of the subject, I was faced with the problem of trying to maintain the aim of promoting critical thinking and promoting group learning and assessment within the reduced resources available to the subject. The group journal was a central strategy – a record of the group learning processes and assessment exercises undertaken by students. The journal would require students to meet as learning groups outside class hours to document their reflections, both individually and as a group, on a variety of projects.

The innovation

I had introduced an individual reflective journal for each student to replace the vagaries of a class performance mark. Students and tutors had complained that a 'class performance' mark was highly subjective, biased against those who refrained from speaking because of shyness or cultural values that emphasize listening and quietness as forms of respect. The journal offered the opportunity for students to develop an original piece of work as proof of their learning and commitment to the subject. Tutors commented on the quality and originality of students' work and the corresponding reduction in plagiarism. However tutors were upset by the increase in the time spent marking the journals and providing feedback to students. Given the budget cuts and increasing student numbers, individual journals could no longer be justified – group work and group journals seemed to provide the answer.

Prior to the introduction of the group journal, the curriculum was altered to reflect the importance of group work and peer learning: 30 per cent of the marks were allocated for group work, including a group presentation (10 per cent) and group journal (20 per cent). A detailed *Guide to Study Groups* was provided for students. This outlined important aspects of study groups – formation, meetings, monitoring and evaluation, stages in the development of groups, giving and receiving feedback. The guide was included in the course materials and its role in developing group-learning skills and in the development of the journal was explained in the introductory lectures and tutorials.

The group journal consisted of two parts: the group record of activities and learning processes (Part A) and the current issues journal (Part B). Part A included a group workbook that would contain individual and group answers to questions set in lectures and workshops, and the group's record of its learning processes and meetings throughout the semester. The lecture and workshop programme was rewritten to incorporate questions for group discussion and group activities, such as institutional visits to courts and the state parliament, which were to be recorded in the journal.

Part B consisted of a number of group reflections and commentary on the content and context of business law in the light of current newspaper and journal articles. These articles were collected from major newspapers, professional journals and the Internet. (To prevent plagiarism all articles had to be selected only from sources published in the current semester.) Part B was incorporated into the workshops as a resource for students and tutors to use as the basis of class discussion and to highlight current legal issues and their relationship to the content of the course. This aspect of the journal proved surprisingly successful and has been adopted as the centrepiece of other subjects' seminar materials. Some tutors have insisted that the reflective commentaries be based on substantial current journal articles as a means of updating their own knowledge!

The learning objectives of reflective journal writing emphasized the need to move beyond recount and summary modes of writing to a dialogue mode of group communication and writing. The journal commenced with the requirement that students undertake an 'approaches to learning' questionnaire and then reflect on their learning both individually and as a group. The questionnaire consisted of questions about learning styles and provided students with an opportunity to reflect on their own learning and the differing approaches to learning within the group.

Students were required to assess and evaluate the journal and the effectiveness of the group throughout the semester. Each group was required to select its best commentary and to explain how the commentary met criteria for critical thinking about legal issues. The assessment and evaluation sheets and the nominated commentary were part of the basis of assessment by the tutor – allowing tutors to go directly to the assessment items within the journal and thus reduce marking time.

The assessment was based on criteria for a pooled mark, set out in the programme, which was to be divided between the group on the basis of the amount of work each member had contributed. This apportionment was decided by the group and indicated at the front of the journal.

Rationale

The rationale for the structure of the journal was to assist students to write, both individually and as a group, about the process of their learning to encourage a deeper, more critical approach to knowledge and to see the law within a social and economic context. The journal writing provided an alternative to the short answer and multiple-choice exams that have become a conventional response to large student numbers and diminishing resources. The current issues journal allowed students to research and write about areas of their own interest and engage in a critical response to views expressed in journals and newspapers. The benefits of group and peer learning are documented elsewhere in these chapters, however a group journal specifically encourages students to reflect and clarify issues and to consider other perspectives when recording and writing up their journal.

At a more basic level, the requirement to read and write about current issues in journal and newspaper articles served three purposes: firstly it assisted students from a non-English-speaking background to read newspapers and journals on a regular basis. There was an urgent need to address the lack of English reading and comprehension skills within the subject. Secondly, for students from overseas, it helped provide some background to the social and economic context in which the law was developing. Finally, it provided a link between the content of the course and 'real world' examples.

The journal also provided a means of integrating lecture and workshop activities, providing a group reflection on the purposes and objectives of the teaching and learning activity and an assessment of its effectiveness. I have changed my own lectures and a number of activities and group tasks as a result of student comments in the group journal!

Implementation

Once the curriculum had been adapted for group learning and the journal incorporated as the centrepiece of assessment for group activities, meetings were held with all lecturers and tutors involved with the subject, to discuss the focus on group learning and the role of the journal. With the participation of some of the editors of this book, we held a workshop on journals for teaching staff together with some readings about reflective journal writing.

Most tutors were encouraging about the changes. They were relieved that, with groups of four to six students, the group journal would substantially reduce marking. There was also general consensus that reading and writing, especially amongst students with non-English-speaking backgrounds, needed to be encouraged and improved if they were to successfully complete the subject and the business degree. However there were the usual concerns with group marking. How were the groups to be selected? How could the free-rider problem be addressed? How could the individual contribution of each member be assessed accurately? What was the basis of the assessment of the journal?

It was decided that we would let the groups self-select for the first semester. However, we emphasized the need for diversity in groups especially an even spread of English language skills and a mix of cultures in each group.

The assessment issues surrounding the journal were a major concern. However, unlike personal reflective journal writing, the group journal in business law was centred on recording specific tasks – the court visit, seminar presentation and the group meetings (to develop and prepare the presentations). Students were advised that they must follow the laws of meeting procedure as to notice, agenda, and a record of the minutes of the meeting.

In Part A therefore, the tutors would look to the form of the meeting process and check that it was reflective of the group seminar presentation, met minimum legal requirements for lawful meetings and all assessment activities had been duly completed and entered into the journal.

In Part B the reflective commentaries would be assessed by considering the commentary nominated by the group and in light of the evaluation and assessment sheet completed by the group and attached to the front of the journal. The evaluation sheet required the group to assess their best commentary in the light of specific academic criteria, such as intellectual coherence, use of primary and secondary sources, relationship of article to the course content.

Group journals have a number of other advantages for teaching and learning in universities. Unlike essays that may be 'recycled' and plagiarized – an increasing problem at all levels of education – the journal required commentaries only on articles published within the current semester, thus minimizing the possibility of plagiarism in this regard. Secondly, because entries in Part A flowed from lecture and workshop questions, these would be changed and adapted each semester to pick up any copying of journals. Finally, as workshops would use articles from the journals in class discussion, tutors could refer to, check and provide formative assessment to the groups to ensure the continuous maintenance of the journal throughout the semester (rather than a desperate write-up the night before it was due).

The meeting of tutors also agreed that group meetings and the timing of group activities and journal tasks should be clearly signposted in course materials. This enabled tutors to collect journals in the middle of the semester knowing that students must have held three meetings and collected three articles and completed the associated commentaries. These signposts were added in bold to course documents and it was agreed that an interim mark should be awarded and students advised how to improve their journals at least once before final submission. To assist in this, some tutors developed a template to facilitate the interim marking and this was generally adopted.

The decision to provide guidance and an interim mark for formative purposes had a major beneficial effect on the students' attention to the journal throughout the semester and improved the quality of the journal entries.

Finally, there was much discussion amongst the tutors as to the use of a pooled mark for the journal and the group's allocation of a mark to each member. Some tutors felt that groups would divide all marks equally to avoid any disputes. Other tutors wanted students to each confidentially allocate marks for the group and the tutor would use these to decide the individual student's mark. Finally it was decided that tutors, as far as possible, would award a mark that could not be divided equally between the group so as to force some acknowledgement of differences in contribution within the group. It was also agreed that tutors would accept the consensus of the group as to division of marks, however in the event of dispute we would ask each student to provide a confidential assessment of the individual student's contribution and use this as the basis of allocation of marks.

I must say I have been surprised by the lack of disputes in the allocation of individual marks and only on a couple of occasions have I been forced to arbitrate the division of the pooled mark.

Perhaps the greatest problem has involved the maintenance of groups in the face of students' withdrawal from the subject. This was especially difficult with groups comprising part-time students. Special consideration has to be given to early warnings about group disintegration and procedures need to be in place to allow for amalgamation and expansion of groups when this problem arises.

Briefing the students

As the coordinator and lecturer in the subject, I was aware that the success of the group learning and journal would depend on the students' reactions and a proper understanding of the aims and objectives of the journal and how it would be assessed. A proper briefing as to the role and importance of the journal, in terms of the course objectives and assessments would be critical to its success.

To introduce the journal, I devoted the first lecture to a consideration of what I (and the university) regarded as essential outcomes for graduates. I emphasized the need for developing critical thinking skills and an understanding of the processes of learning as the most important goals of the subject. I then explained the educational benefits of group learning and the importance of communication and group interaction in the learning process.

The role of the journal as a means of recording reflections of the learning within the group and the Part B project requiring selection of articles for reflection and critical comment was explained in detail. Students were advised that they could self-select the members of their group; however it was stressed that groups should be culturally diverse and we expected heterogeneous groups. The groups would be organized in each workshop in week three after an ice-breaking exercise.

I was initially surprised at the positive feedback from the first lecture. Students seemed to enjoy an introduction to a subject through a discussion of the approach to teaching and learning that would be adopted in the subject. Many had never considered what the 'critical thinking' buzzword meant and I think the use of the 'approaches to learning' questionnaire triggered discussion and thinking about each student's own approach to learning. A student stated that, although he had been studying at university for two years, this was the first time he had thought about what teaching and learning actually meant!

Feedback

At the end of the academic year, after a trial of the journal for two semesters, I sought feedback from tutors and students. The tutors enjoyed student journals where the students had authentically engaged in the journal writing tasks, especially the reflections on the learning and teaching process. It was interesting for all teaching staff to share the good and bad comments about our teaching and what students did and did not like about the course.

Most tutors agreed that there were benefits in the use of the journal and that it should be retained in a modified form. Tutors commented on the great reduction in marking load by according a pooled group mark for the journal and requiring students to divide the mark between themselves. They also saw the journal as a way of monitoring student activity outside class hours and encouraging greater learning. Tutors found that the best journals provided interesting articles for discussion in workshops and were an important stimulus to discussion. Other tutors, who were more focused on the content and continued to lecture in the workshop, did not provide sufficient feedback or encouragement to support the group journals. As a result the group journals in these workshops were of a poorer standard.

However, tutors were concerned about the lack of diversity in groups. Students from the same cultural backgrounds automatically chose to work together. One tutor recounted the story of an Indonesian student who was in a group with all Hong Kong Chinese – the group only ever communicated in Cantonese throughout the semester and she was totally excluded. Other tutors were frustrated by groups that collapsed during the course of the semester – some students disappeared or refused to work with others. Such situations caused problems for assessment and marking. Tutors were also concerned about complaints from highly motivated students, who felt they were carrying the group and their marks were suffering. Most groups refused to give differential marks to members because of concerns about hurting others and feelings of group solidarity. The group presentation of seminar questions often broke down to individual students preparing a question each and hoping it would be all right on the day.

The student feedback and assessment sheets required for the journal provided further insights into the success of the project. Many students simply hated the idea of keeping a journal and the need to write reflectively about their group's learning. Too often the writing became very pro forma and it appeared students were merely 'going through the motions' in recording the learning process. Despite the briefing at the beginning of each semester the articles students collected were often unsuitable and the commentaries amounted to little more than a summary of the article. There was also evidence of plagiarism of other groups' journals and recycling of the answers to seminar questions, meeting agendas and articles between groups in different workshops.

The most common complaint from students was the amount of time and effort in writing and maintaining the journal – most argued it should be worth at least 50 per cent of the marks for the subject. Other students were concerned how the journal was marked, especially given the number of tutors and the differing approaches to marking. Some tutors marked Part A on the format that if each task and the record of group meetings was included then full marks were given. Other tutors read the journal carefully and graded all journals. The assessment of Part B also varied because of the wide range in the quality of journals and the differing expectations of tutors. The variation in marking was resolved by the development of a markers' template. Originally developed by one tutor as a quick way of marking and giving feedback, it was adopted by nearly all tutors and has since been modified to include more information for feedback purposes.

Reforming the journal

Most tutors agreed that the group journal should be maintained but that there was a need to rethink carefully the role of the journal to make it less burdensome on students, while focusing more deeply on peer learning and the educational outcomes for the group. The tutors agreed on the need for improvement in a number of vital areas: the selection and maintenance of the groups, the refinement of the group tasks in the journal to assist in developing critical thinking, the integration of the journal into the workshops. Tutors also acknowledged that the group journal required them to change their role in workshops to that of facilitators. A greater involvement in assisting groups, providing continuous formative assessment throughout the semester and encouraging the development of the journal were seen as important ways that tutors could assist in maintaining the journal as an important part of the subject.

A number of reforms were made to improve the journal. The instructions in the course materials were expanded to include an overview of critical thinking using the analogy of 'knowledge as design' and students were asked to consider the structure, purpose and assumptions behind each article rather than merely summarizing. The best articles from the previous semester were included to highlight what was expected. Tutors used these articles and modelled the type of analysis that was expected in the commentaries.

The journal instructions were rewritten to clearly delineate individual and group tasks. In order to balance the assessment regime, certain projects recorded in the journal became individual work – the court report and the reflection on the student's past learning experience were recorded individually in the journal. Students were also asked to develop a 'critical legal incident' analysis of some legal event in their own lives and to analyse and critique the events and people involved. These individual tasks were more highly focused on critical thinking and helped balance the marks between group and individual assessment. Students who believed that their group mark did not reflect their effort could request tutors to consider their individual efforts.

In order to improve the workshops, the assigned questions were re-written. Drawing on my study of critical thinking, I tried to construct a developmental sequence of questions that moved from concrete to more abstract concepts. The aim was to give students practice in a workable problem-solving process and provide a variety of differing questions to maintain interest and motivation. Rather than simple problem solving, questions involved developing policy statements on law, writing philosophic justifications for legal argument and analysis of contracts and drafting exercises. The seminar problems were no longer incorporated in the journal, unless students were required to resubmit their work, in which case the changes had to be documented. To further complement student involvement a new class performance regime was introduced. A self-assessment form was developed for class performance in the workshop to establish the criteria for students to understand what was required (annex A). The form allowed students to self-assess their participation based on examples of their performance throughout the semester.

Rather than continue using the journal as a record of the learning process, specific reflective questions were addressed to the group requiring them to focus on their learning strategies and methods and a major project was introduced as the focus of Part A. The major group project was the writing of a final exam for the subject. This project required each group to prepare a final exam containing ten multiple choice questions, two short answer questions and two problem questions. Model answers and an analysis of the questions in terms of how the exam met the subject's aims and objectives were also required. I felt that to create the final exam was a powerful strategy for encouraging critical thinking about the course and would be more effective and easier for tutors to assess than the record of the group's learning.

Part B of the journal – the critical commentaries – was retained. Such an exercise builds bridges between academic study and the 'real world', providing students with practical applications of their studies and fostering a critical attitude to the media. However the number of articles was reduced and emphasis was placed on critical evaluation rather than summary. Tutors were instructed to refer to the articles and use them as the basis for class discussion. By incorporating the articles and the group commentaries, students were forced to maintain the journal and received regular feedback as to the quality of their work.

In my opinion, the mix of the journal, between individual and group work, between development of group maintenance skills and the substantive tasks involving the group learning, the content of the subject and the proportion of the assessment the journal carries in the overall assessment regime, is crucial to its success. The readjustment of the journal provided a greater focus on the process of group learning and reduced the quantity of work whilst emphasizing the need for greater depth.

I circulated marks of all tutors for the journal assessments for comparison. This had the effect of dramatically tightening the range of tutors' marks. Marking was also tightened by the use of marking sheets and student evaluation forms, which clearly indicated the aims and objectives of the project and the basis for assessment.

The groups were no longer self-selecting. In order to encourage diversity and equality amongst groups, each group was required to have a minimum of 2,000km between all the group members' place of birth, and all native

English speakers had to be spread across the groups. These rules had the effect of culturally diverse groups with roughly the same level of English competence in each group. Finally it was required that English was the lingua franca for all group meetings.

Division of the pooled mark still remained a matter of contention. However I developed a form (annexed as B) to allow each individual to assess the other group members confidentially and then allow a ratio to be developed. This seemed to partly resolve the free rider issue.

Conclusion

The journal is still a work in progress. Since its introduction the subject has faced further challenges with increasing student numbers, and pressure to expand the content of the subject to cover the rapid growth of law. Tutorials have expanded to 30 to 35 students. The larger group numbers have meant that the groups become unwieldy and difficult. However, the use of group work and the journal projects still provide an important focus for critical thinking about the law and a strategy for developing self-directed cooperative learners. Students have found it difficult initially to work cooperatively within groups, but once this reluctance has been overcome many students have reported on their growing understanding of the opinions and views of other students. This has led to continuing informal group learning throughout their degree and the development of long-term personal relationships. For me, this is perhaps the most important and unexpected outcome.

The chapter has not canvassed the strong educational and sociological evidence in support of group learning. Suffice to say it develops teamwork, an increased awareness of the importance of cooperative effort, and an understanding of group dynamics and interpersonal relations. Learning in groups is not merely a matter of learning about the skills and concepts of a subject discipline, but it is also a vehicle for learning about groups: developing abilities in cooperative work for later life. In my subject the group journal has been a central part of group learning and assessment.

CLASS PERFORMANCE RATING FORM

STUDENT NAME: —————————————— OVERALL RATING: ——————————

Circle a number for each question.

1. On <u>one</u> of the following charts, note the quality of contribution to class discussion (quality is defined by factors such as whether contributions operated as a stimulus to discussion or added to the general success of the class).

    (a) One of the most frequent contributors (extrovert)

    low quality   high quality
    ....

    1   2   3   4   5   6   7   8   9   10

    (b) A fairly frequent contributor (addresses the class at least once per week)

    low quality   high quality
    ....

    1   2   3   4   5   6   7   8   9   10

    (c) An infrequent contributor (quiet/active listener)

    low quality   high quality
    ....

    1   2   3   4   5   6   7   8   9   10

    Give one example of contribution:

2. On <u>one</u> of the following charts, rate the frequency and effectiveness of the student's attempts to clarify for others points which arose in discussion.

    (a) One of the most frequent contributors

    ineffective   highly effective
    ....

    1   2   3   4   5   6   7   8   9   10

    (b) A fairly frequent contributor

    ineffective   highly effective
    ....

    1   2   3   4   5   6   7   8   9   10

    (c) An infrequent contributor

    ineffective   highly effective
    ....

    1   2   3   4   5   6   7   8   9   10

3. Rate the quality of the preparation for class.

    poor   fairly effective   excellent
    ....

    1   2   3   4   5   6   7   8   9   10

4. Rate the extent to which contributions to class facilitated discussion (eg comments and questions extended the point under discussion), or were unhelpful and hindered discussion.

    hindering/unhelpful   helpful   excellent
    ....

    1   2   3   4   5   6   7   8   9   10

5. Indicate how frequently this student contributed a novel and perceptive point of view during class discussions.

    never   sometimes   frequently
    ....

    1   2   3   4   5   6   7   8   9   10

6. Indicate how logically presented this student's arguments were in class presentation and under questioning from students and tutor.

usually confused				sometimes logical					very logical

....

| 1 | 2 | 3 | 4 | 5 | 6 | 7 | 8 | 9 | 10 |

7. Indicate how well this student managed to develop and answer questions and argue points of law from different perspectives.

little or no ability				fairly well					very well

....

| 1 | 2 | 3 | 4 | 5 | 6 | 7 | 8 | 9 | 10 |

8. Improvement in oral expression in class discussion is:

poor				good					excellent

....

| 1 | 2 | 3 | 4 | 5 | 6 | 7 | 8 | 9 | 10 |

9. On the basis of contributions to class discussion, rate how well motivated this student is:

uninterested								keen and motivated	

....

| 1 | 2 | 3 | 4 | 5 | 6 | 7 | 8 | 9 | 10 |

10. General rating of class performance and written work. In comparison with the rest of the group, this student is:

poor				good					excellent

....

| 1 | 2 | 3 | 4 | 5 | 6 | 7 | 8 | 9 | 10 |

For overall rating add all questions (out of 100): ....%

PEER ASSESSMENT
INDIVIDUAL'S CONTRIBUTION TO GROUP PROJECT

STUDENT NAME: ———————————————

The mark awarded to the group shall be weighted in accordance with the assessment of the contribution of each individual member, according to the criteria set out below. The ability to assess your colleagues accurately is an important skill. Take time to rate each member of your group objectively and without bias. All individual responses will be kept confidential.

For each member of the group, including yourself, award a mark out of 5 for the level of participation in each of the tasks listed in the table. Enter your responses using the following grading:

1   Did not contribute in any way
2   Small level of contribution/willing but not very successful
3   Average
4   Above average
5   Outstanding

Group member	1.	2.	3.	4.	5.
(a) Legal research					
(b) Reading and analysis issues					
(c) Developing arguments and conclusions					
(d) Writing the report/preparing material for presentation					
(e) Presentation					
(f) Other criteria?					

9

Autonomy, uncertainty and peer learning in IT project work

Brian Lederer and Richard Raban

. . . within teams who know how to dialogue. . . collective
intelligence rises to become much higher than the brightest member
of the team. However, in teams where individuals compete to be
right and have the last say, the collective intelligence falls below the
level of the least bright team member because the brighter members
begin to cancel each other out with power plays and intimidation.
(McGee-Cooper, 1998)

Autonomy

Here's a recent snatch of conversation that opens up some of the issues. It's
between a student and a lecturer. They are talking about the software
development case study (SDCS) that the student had completed the previous
year:

Lecturer: How are you going – you were one of the students who
had a problem with clarity?

Student: Yes. I'm fine – I've just got a couple of subjects to finish
off. How's SDCS going this year?

Lecturer: Not bad. But we've still got problems of clarity with the
guidelines. Ironically, it wasn't just in your year; last year,
when I coordinated, uncertainty was again an issue –

	probably even more so than what you experienced! I think it's partly tied up with the tensions involved in trying to promote autonomy – we're trying to give students the freedom to do things their own way. But then we have to assess them so the guidelines have to be clear.
Student:	So the conflicts are unavoidable?
Lecturer:	I'm not sure. This year we seem to have been working towards the idea of making the criteria *generic*. Requiring that the deliverables have certain quality features or that the groups adopt certain processes, such as Q/A or testing. Maybe this is a way out.

Likewise, from a current SDCS student:

Student:	Yes, SDCS simulates an industrial environment if you mean the worst kind of industrial environment. It's impossible to meet the needs of a customer who does not know what he wants or refuses to articulate what he wants.

Autonomy for the students is a design goal for SDCS. It is a foundation subject in the BSc (Computing) degree and has been offered for five years now. This type of subject, where the aim is to simulate the workplace environment (and not just the 'worst aspects of it'!) is becoming popular (Bryant, 1999; Shaw and Tomayko, 1991). In SDCS students engage, in teams of seven, with a year-long project intended to be large enough to require them to have to collaborate; that is, it would be impossible for one student to complete all the work on his or her own. Students have to bring to bear skills acquired from the rest of the degree – technical, communication, and managerial – and, hopefully, this gives them a sense of completion by 'bringing it altogether'. Autonomy means that the teams can choose their own members, the project from those on offer, and how they go about it. That is, they choose the design methodologies, programming languages, and so on. But periodically they have to submit a deliverable – such as a design document or a code demonstration – for assessment. For each deliverable the students are given a list of requirements ('what we want') and guidelines ('how you will be marked'). But, as the conversations above show, there are still uncertainties – either by design or accident on the coordinator's part. Some of this uncertainty can be resolved by the teams in discussion with their tutors, but, at the end of the day, there is greater residual uncertainty than the students have been used to in previous project-based subjects.

Uncertainty

The students are understandably concerned about what is expected of them: they want to know what they have to do to get good marks to pass the subject. But the lecturers – sphynx like, as it sometimes appears to the students – will comply only so far: they actually want the students to learn to cope with uncertainty because they see this as characterizing the workplace environment.

Students might say:'this is fine as far as "how to do it" goes; but we've got a right to know *what* we have to do and *how* we'll be marked'. Ideally this is true: the coordinator should be absolutely clear about what is to be done and the guidelines for assessing it; the students, for their part, should figure out how it will be done. In support of this, the students will claim that in industry you receive clear requirements: these are hammered out with the client. However, if pressed, some students will give a less simple view. For example, one part-time student project leader acknowledged that although, in his company, requirements for large projects were well determined it was a different story for small projects, where there was often a lot of uncertainty about what was required.

Colleagues, especially those who have worked in industry, will also acknowledge that there is often uncertainty in projects, both about what has to be done as well as how it will be done. Unlike the design for a house, say, total clarity at the outset is something of a myth. Although, at that stage, a *gestalt* for the system as a whole might exist in someone's mind, a lot of important detail will only emerge – often in consultation with the client, users, or other stakeholders – as the project evolves. It can also emerge from 'environmental' changes: as the communications or database systems, for example, change. This uncertainty is recognized by prototyping methodologies, in which the team builds a cut down version of the system – implementing only a subset of the requirements – and then checks it out with the client. The use of such prototyping is a promising approach for SDCS despite mixed experience so far. Also promising is the provision of a genuine external client and this year we tried this out with four of the twenty-four teams.

But most of the teams, in their efforts to reduce uncertainty, have to fall back on the coordinator or liaison officer as proxies for a client. And it is here that we have to deal with another source of uncertainty that some colleagues are prepared to admit: their own uncertainty when designing or supervising senior project work. In proposing projects that are relevant to students the risk academics take is that they go beyond their own expertise. This is especially true when, as in SDCS, we have part-time students who are working in industry and employing the latest techniques with which the academics may not be familiar. How much of his or her own ignorance can the academic reveal without losing credibility? This is somehow tied up with the student-centred rather than teacher-directed learning we are trying to promote in SDCS. Not all students can handle this. One of the authors had the experience recently of floundering in a tutorial in a junior subject: he had not prepared for one of the questions in the last tutorial and got into trouble trying to work through the solution. This was obvious to the small class, all but one of whom left, possibly in disgust. The remaining student, a bright mature-aged student, struggled on with the tutor: they were both in it together. At one point the student said: 'this is the first time I've experienced engagement at UTS'.

Peer learning

How does peer learning come in here? The hope is that, as students collaborate to reduce uncertainty through finding out what they have to do and how to do it, sharing of knowledge and skills will go on. We say 'hope' because, from observation or anecdote, it is clear that the opportunities for peer learning are not always realized. We see the relationship between autonomy and peer learning as follows: autonomy, by providing a space in which the team can make its own adjustments, free from uninvited intervention by the lecturer, is a precondition for peer learning. Students need to exercise some degree of autonomy before they can learn effectively with and from each other. Autonomy therefore serves an educational, as well as an industrial, goal. Through acting autonomously, students feel responsible for the outcome. This is motivating and releases energy. This shows up in some of the reports where students, although complaining about the pain of the subject, say that it was one of their best learning experiences. However, autonomy entails risks, as we shall see.

This business of 'freedom to make adjustments' brings in the important concept of *variety*. To explore this concept, consider a simple model of a tutorial. Groups of students are working on a problem. The tutor is walking around the room and monitoring what they are doing. By interaction the tutor discovers that many groups have the same difficulty and goes to the board to share this with the class. The tutor does not give away the solution but just enough information so that the students can progress beyond the breakpoint.

In a previous paper (Lederer et al., 2000) we analysed this tutorial model from the perspective of variety. In lecture mode the variety of the students (number of states they can be in) has to be cut down to match that of the lecturer so that learning (the 'essential variable') can take place: hence the need for 'variety attenuating' rules (no talking, no walking) and prerequisites (all students are assumed to be in roughly the same state of readiness). This exemplifies Ashby's principle of 'requisite variety' (Ashby, 1956; Beer, 1974): for a system (class here) to be in control, the variety of the regulated part (students) must not exceed that of the regulating part (teacher). Otherwise, essential variables will go out of limits. An example would be fencing: I have requisite variety if I can parry every move my opponent makes; then the essential variable (my blood volume!) remains within limits. Likewise, a pilot has requisite variety if every wind gust can be matched by a movement of the controls (ailerons, and so forth) so as to control the essential variables – plane on course and passengers comfortable. In each case, the regulating part of the total system is said to *absorb* the variety of the regulated part.

Applying this to teaching we can say that, in tutorial mode, the students are permitted larger variety than in lecture mode (because we relax the rules) but the lecturer's variety remains unchanged. Ashby's law is obeyed here because now the students themselves (rather than the rules) absorb one another's variety through peer learning interactions. Breakpoints come about when the students get stuck and the tutor has to intervene. This should be a manageable task for the tutor – his or her variety for intervening (and monitoring) is requisite.

We have an analogous situation in SDCS although one that is more complex. One obvious case is that of the teams working on the guidelines and getting stuck: they can raise this at a meeting with their liaison officer (acting like a tutor) who will hopefully be able to give a clarification or seek one from the coordinator.

Obstacles to peer learning

There are other ways in which the team can get stuck – and this shows the risks associated with autonomy. Here are some examples.

> *Two students.* We're worried. There's a big conflict in our group. We two are having to do all the technical work. The other two are footballer types and will bash us up if we complain.

> *A bright student (team member).* In my experience one or two techos (out of seven students) dominated in SDCS; in SD&D [software design and development; a second year project-based subject] it was one out of ten. In the latter case the student used a language [Perl]

that the rest of us didn't know. That student dictated to the designers and documentors. Not all students got involved: either because of apathy, mistaken belief in 'trickle down', desire to get out of the subject lightly, or pressure from other areas – job or social life. In my opinion companies will employ such students – the demand for IT people is that intense.

Student's report at the end of the year. Our project leader behaved like 'the evil prince': he hogged most of the interesting work for himself and his two other mates. The rest of us, though technically competent, couldn't get any interesting work.

Team to liaison officer. You're asking us why we give equal shares to all members on the work breakdown sheet [teams are required to submit such a sheet with each deliverable giving, for each team member, their percentage contribution to the work and, hence, their share of the marks]. Well this way we preserve harmony in the group.

Student project leader on peer learning. We were fortunate to get a couple of good technical people who were part of the programming group. There was probably some peer learning going on in that group. But there was not much learning amongst the others including myself [project leader]. There was little time for it with all the pressures to get the deliverables in, other subjects, etc.

Student project leader on peer learning. No, there wasn't much peer learning going on. The roles of documentor, Q/A person, and programmer were clear-cut and filled by people who already knew what to do. At most there would have been some peer learning amongst the programmers because there were some new things going on there.

These conversations highlight the following dysfunctions:

- formation of cliques – either at the technical or managerial level;
- unwillingness to honestly credit work contribution;
- choosing a team made up of friends rather than one giving a good mix of skills;
- excessive pressure to get the job done;
- getting locked into fixed roles.

Learning organizations

How can we offset these dysfunctions? In the next section, we attempt to analyse the peer learning situation and some of the above problems and, in the final section, we consider a tool for helping students monitor work contributions. But we need something stronger if we're going to get the students onside: a culture that values peer learning and appreciates its relevance. At a recent conference, one of the participants described his job as a facilitator: going into organizations and trying to effect a change to *learning organizations*: organizations where the employees are cooperative rather than competitive, share knowledge and skills, engage in inquiry, and so forth (Senge, 1990). The quotation at the beginning of this chapter from McGee-Cooper captures the spirit of this. Of course, the reason companies are interested is partly pragmatic: if the employees can teach one another, this reduces the cost of training. If this is the environment that students are going into, then we have an additional motivator: peer learning can be promoted as not just part of the educational experience at university, but as a process that may continue on into industry.

Analysis

We now want to go into some of the issues raised above in greater detail combining theoretical perspectives from the literature with reflections based on our experience; in particular, we want to look at some of the dysfunctions touched on above. We look at the group as a whole and view the set of interactions as a complex system behaving dynamically. Initial conditions involve team formation. As the team interacts in carrying out the work involved in the deliverables we look at the role of the liaison officer in monitoring group dynamics.

Earlier chapters in this book have defined peer learning. Here we want to look at the opportunities for peer learning in an IT project setting with lots of interactions. To this end we begin with a model of the unit of interaction: two students teaching one another.

Laurillard's conversational model of peer learning

According to this model (Laurillard, 1993) peer learning entails a two-way *conversational* process. Academic learning is seen as discursive process between participants whose roles are 'teacher' and 'student', it being understood that, in the context of peer learning, the teacher role is taken by a student (Laurillard, 1993: 103). In the model there are two levels of interaction. At the bottom level (action or task level) the student acts to achieve the task goal and receives *intrinsic* (automatic) feedback from an experiential environment provided by the teacher (for example, the student interacts with some apparatus or software system). At the top level (description, conceptual, or theoretical level) the student offers descriptions of or, alternatively, *reflections* upon, his or her task level experience and receives *extrinsic* feedback from the teacher: re-descriptions, critical comments, and so forth. The model incorporates *adaptation* in that the teacher can modify the task goal in the light of the student's description such as when the student shows a misconception; likewise, students can modify their task action in the light of the teacher's comments so as to achieve the goal more effectively. It often helps if the roles are reversed and the person originally taking the student role tries to teach the concepts to the other person thereby exposing conflicts (misconceptions, contradictions, and so forth) the resolution of which, in the form of *agreements*, results in understanding: this role reversal is termed *teachback* (Laurillard, 1993: 190).

But peer learning is not a panacea. As Laurillard remarks (Laurillard, 1993: 72):

> Discussion between students is an excellent partial method of learning that needs to be complemented by something offering the other characteristics, if students are not to flounder in mutually progressive ignorance.

Team formation

When they form we encourage teams to choose their members wisely, bearing in mind the team's need for a variety of skills to match that required by the project. For example, a project might require an analyst with a certain amount of experience in design work (say three years) and a certain level of skill (say 'intermediate') in a particular design methodology; likewise, it might be determined that there should be two Java programmers of at least two years experience, with one capable of taking a lead role. This skills mix would have to be compared with that determined by the task. In an industrial setting one aims at getting as good a match as possible.

What happens if there *is* a gap? Presumably, in an industrial setting, one speculates about the ability of the team itself to close the gap by subsequent individual or, indeed, peer learning: in other words, by learning on the job. Alternatively, one considers supplementary training. In either case, one is considering the potential for the gap to be made up by team learning of one kind or another. This seems to argue that, in forming a team whose initial mix falls short of that required, one should also consider 'generic skills' for teaching and/or learning to go on within the team. This we might term the team's 'learning potential'. This would include the potential for individual learning as well as peer learning. The focus here is on conditions for realizing the latter potential.

Dynamics

Suppose, in the SDCS situation, a team has formed with a mix of skills that falls short of that required but that there is a good potential for peer learning. For example, in the above case it is found that although one student programmer's knowledge of Java is poor, the other student's knowledge is quite good. In a mechanical analogy, we might imagine that the team at the time of formation is like a ball placed near the lip of a basin and ready to roll to the bottom. In this analogy the ball's initial height corresponds to the learning potential. In the present example this potential is good because one student has a skill that the other lacks but needs in order to carry out the task. Then the rolling of the ball corresponds to peer learning dynamics, and the equilibrium state at the bottom to some state of shared knowledge (relative to the task).

What can upset the learning dynamics? One possible problem is interference by teachers – be they, in the SDCS situation, coordinator or liaison officer. This problem has been analysed in Robinson (1979). In Robinson's analysis the team is regarded as a complex system (not a collection of individuals) with its own set of relationships and its own dynamics. Learning is seen to occur as a byproduct of this system 'running to equilibrium'. By this it is meant that, provided there is no obstruction, learning does not have to be teacher directed but will tend to occur automatically as a result of group dynamics – as a result of one member responding to the needs of another. Information will reverberate through the system: at one stage in this process a student (A) might be teaching another student (B); at another stage the roles might be reversed (B teaching A; alternatively, B might teach C). A student alternates between being, as tutee, a generator of variety (for example, asking questions) and, as tutor, an absorber of variety (for example, giving answers).

Ironically, the conditions for good peer learning dynamics to occur are almost completely the opposite to those required for lecture mode. For lecturing to work it is necessary to assume class homogeneity (low student variety): because all students are to receive identical (broadcast) input from the lecturer it is necessary that they all be in the same state of readiness. But for the kind of interactive learning of interest here to occur, variety amongst the students is actually necessary: if students are to teach one another we actually require the team to be heterogeneous in terms of its knowledge and skills (we require the team to have learning potential). Perhaps A has a skill that B lacks and vice versa. Then there can be some sharing: the team will mobilize its own variety of its own accord. That is, it is self-organizing. For this to happen, the teacher (liaison officer) needs to step right back otherwise the team's reflex will be to ask for help. Another way of saying this is that if the team is to find its own equilibrium, it needs freedom from interference or constraint. A similar remark applies to the team's task-oriented, as distinct from learning, activity. If it is to reach equilibrium – now consensus – it needs to be free of interference. This was our thesis – the need for the teams to be self-managing, not just because this simulates the industrial situation but also because it is a precondition for peer learning.

Role of liaison officer

So, if peer learning requires a team to exhibit autonomy, why have the liaison officer involved at all? The main reason is because internal constraints, of the team's own making, can also militate against good learning dynamics. We have in mind dysfunctions in group processes such as the formation of cliques. Sometimes it can happen that a nucleus of 'techos' forms (the 'guru' syndrome): the nucleus hogs the juicy parts (the main design and programming work) and relegates tasks like quality assurance or documentation to the rest of the team. The nucleus may see itself as simply wanting to expedite the project or obtain good marks and it may judge the rest of the team, in some cases correctly, as 'hangers on'. The rest of the team, for their part, may perceive the nucleus as being on a power trip and may be concerned about this. Or, if indeed they are hangers on, the rest of the team may not care what the nucleus does so long as they get the requisite share of the marks. Then the team may be fantastically productive and may, within the nucleus, experience individual learning; but it fails to realize the potential for peer learning. Vice versa, 'management-heavies' may force the 'techos' to do the actual work: again, not much learning (this time within the nucleus). It is here that the liaison officer, in detecting such conditions and feeding them back to the team, can play a valuable role in promoting good dynamics. The liaison officer might perhaps point out that the balance between task-oriented and relationship-oriented behaviour has been lost and, also, the advantages to be had from restoring it (as alluded to by McGee-Cooper).

But suppose the internal constraints are not an issue, that there is no external interference (by the teacher), and that the team progresses successfully to equilibrium. This does not necessarily mean that the team can complete the task. It may well be that, despite the peer learning potential being realized, the team's mix of skills still falls short of what is required. Then the team is blocked (in danger of 'floundering in mutually progressive ignorance' – to use Laurillard's phrase). This may show up as a set of questions to the liaison officer – for example 'how are we supposed to use collaboration diagrams in the UML?'

Here the liaison officer can play a 'complementing' role in putting the team in touch with resources (such as books) or can feed the team's state back to the coordinator. Perhaps this is a blockage common to a number of teams (or the whole class) and backup lectures are required (there is provision for this within the SDCS lecture schedule where we run two streams of lectures – one on theory, and the other on project work).

Measurement tool and future work

We mentioned the disinclination teams have to record honest breakdowns of work contributions to a deliverable. At the time of submitting the breakdown, just prior to return of marks, it is too hard to sort out accurate percentages (because this has been forgotten and there are no data available); so it's better to settle for equal percentages than get into conflict. Besides, the team has formed from friends. Then, why not go for an easy ride? Why bother with peer learning?

To get over this problem we have developed a tool for assessing the contributions of individual team members to a deliverable. Requirements for the tool were that individual performances be recorded both quantitatively and qualitatively, immediately after the claimed work was done, and openly (so that all team members can verify individual claims). As implemented the tool requires that students record, on a weekly basis, their time spent on project tasks. Also, on a weekly basis, the team distributes amongst itself a pool of marks to reflect the value of their individual efforts. This weekly pool of marks remains fixed for the project and is weighted by the total number of hours the team spends in each week. For example, the weight associated with a week in which the team worked 100 hours would be twice as big as that for a week involving only 50 hours. (This recognizes that contributions build up as the deadline is approached.) Timeliness of record keeping is enforced by requiring that time spent and performance marks be entered by a set deadline, say by Wednesday of the following week. All team members have access to the records and can monitor their performance at any time to see how they rate compared with the rest of the team. The statistics are not directly used for marking; but there is a strong pressure on the team to allocate percentages that do not entirely ignore the performance figures.

Acknowledgements

We would like to express thanks, for advice and presentations, to the following individuals at UTS: Jenny Edwards, Faculty of Information Technology; Jane Sampson, School of Adult Education, and Kaye Remington, Faculty of Design and Building. We would also like to thank Anna Reid, Institute for Interactive Media and Learning, for advice.

References

Ashby, W (1956) *An Introduction to Cybernetics*, Methuen, London
Beer, S (1974) *Designing Freedom*, Wiley, New York
Bryant, R (1999) Software engineering for seniors: overcoming the administrative fears. *Proceedings of the thirtieth SIGCSE technical symposium on computer science education SIGCSE'99*. ACM Digital Library (http://www.acm.org/pubs/contents/proceedings/cse/299649/p83-bryant/p83-bryant.pdf)
Laurillard, D (1993) *Rethinking University Teaching*, Routledge, London
Lederer, B, Plekhanova, V and Jay, C (2000) Teaching a capstone subject in computing science: a variety engineering approach, *Proceedings of the 23rd Computer Science Conference ACSC2000, Australian Computer Science Communications*, **22** (1), pp 136–42, IEEE Computer Society, The Printing House, Canberra

McGee-Cooper, A (1998) Accountability as covenant: The taproot of servant-leadership in *Insights on Leadership: Service, stewardship, spirit, and servant-leadership* (ed) L Spears, Wiley, New York

Robinson, M (1979) Classroom control: some cybernetic comments on the possible and the impossible, *Journal of Instructional Science*, **8**, pp 369–92

Senge, P (1990) *The Fifth Discipline*, Doubleday, New York

Shaw, M and Tomayko, J (1991) Models for undergraduate project courses in software engineering, in *Software Engineering Education (Proceedings of the Fifth SEI Conference on Software Engineering Education)* (ed) J Tomayko, pp 33–71, Springer-Verlag, Pittsburgh

10

Peer learning using computer supported roleplay-simulations

Robert McLaughlan and Denise Kirkpatrick

An important aspect of higher education is the development of skills that will enable students to function effectively as lifelong learners. In recent years, there has been pressure for university courses to develop in students not only discipline-specific knowledge and skills but also work and life skills such as teamwork, decision making, leadership, communication and negotiation.

Professionally oriented education seeks to cater to a more diverse group of learners, coming from a variety of educational and employment backgrounds. As more university students study part time whether by choice or economic necessity, universities are seeking to respond to student demand for more flexibility in choice of time and place of study by providing flexible alternatives to conventional face-to-face classes. These alternatives may include the use of distance education study materials in a variety of media or the use of Internet-based teaching and learning environments supported by communications technologies.

In this chapter we describe the use of roleplay-simulations that are designed to develop student communication, negotiation and decision-making skills, specific discipline knowledge and provide flexibility for learners through the use of computer-mediated communications and an online learning environment. We do this in the context of an innovative activity that brings together students from different disciplines and different stages of their study to teach about the social, political, economic and scientific dimensions of decision making in different contexts.

Roleplays and simulations

Roleplay-simulations (McLaughlan and Kirkpatrick, 1998) combine the attributes of both simulations and roleplays where participants adopt a functional role or persona within a simulated environment or scenario. They are problem-based units of learning set in motion by a particular task, issue, policy, incident, crisis or problem. The simulation may be designed so that the problems that are to be addressed by participants are either implicit or explicit. Participants learn about the person or role, problem and/or the situation specific to the subject area as a consequence of the interaction between participants in their personae and the scenario (Errington, 1997). Roleplay simulations can be designed to create learning environments that immerse learners in authentic learning. The roleplay simulations that are the subject of this chapter involve groups or classes of university students adopting roles within scenarios and, within these roles, working together to resolve issues and tackle discipline-related problems. The roleplay-simulations with which we have been involved are designed to familiarize participants with the complexities of decision making and negotiation while developing substantive subject knowledge. Within roleplay simulations students learn from and with each other, bringing subject and generic expertise to the scenario and developing understanding and skills as a consequence of their interactions with each other, the scenario and the subject content.

Peer learning in electronic environments

Traditionally most peer learning, whether through roleplay, simulation or another approach, has occurred in formal or informal settings where learners are in close physical proximity to each other. Recently there has been interest in the use of communication technologies such as e-mail to support role-play-simulation interactions, and the Internet as an environment for the creation of simulation scenarios and incidents. The emergence of new learning environments facilitated by communications technologies raises questions regarding how well the principles of collaborative and peer learning that apply in face-to-face settings translate to online learning environments where distributed learners no longer meet in person. Can peer learning be effectively established in the new learning environments created by new technologies?

New communications technologies certainly appear to provide the means by which some previous problems associated with establishing peer and collaborative learning environments may be overcome. They can allow flexibility in learning activities by fostering participation that would otherwise be problematic because of constraints associated with distance, time or the financial cost of attending a face-to-face meeting. Additionally, the anonymity afforded by the electronic environment and the use of pseudonyms can support the adoption of roles and personae. The use of the online environment can allow extended simulation that more closely parallels the timeframes of professional practice, rather than the compressed timescale offered by most face-to-face simulations. This can allow participants greater time for reflection upon simulation content during the interactive phase as well as the incorporation into the simulation of tasks that require additional or external resources. Providing the roleplay simulation online can offer a means of creating educationally rewarding learning experiences in a cost-effective, flexible and realistic manner.

Computer supported roleplay-simulations

In this chapter we are focusing on two computer-supported roleplay-simulations (CSRS) that have been effective in facilitating student learning in different university courses. The two CSRS share common essential phases that fulfil important pedagogical functions while supporting students through the processes of entering the simulated scenario, engaging in interactions and achieving resolution. The two CSRS described here are components of subjects that comprise university courses. In both cases the roleplay simulations are accompanied by lectures, tutorials or independent learning materials associated with the subject. Whilst individual CSRS will include different specific activities designed to relate to the content of the simulation, core features of the structure and design are consistent.

There are four phases of the activity: briefing, interaction, the forum event and reflection. During the *briefing phase* participants become familiar with the structure of the CSRS and the technologies associated with the activity. Personae based on real or fictional identities are allocated to or chosen by participants. Personae may be shared among several participants who must collaborate to act as one character within the scenario. Participants collaborate to research the shared role, negotiate the goals and strategies of the persona and develop a role profile that comprises specific background material on the persona and goals. A position paper covering both specific and general information relating to the persona and its relationship to the context involved in the CSRS may be developed and this may be done individually or collaboratively. This serves to familiarize participants with issues that are likely to arise in the course of events and provide a knowledge base from which they can act.

The *interaction phase* comprises the major activity within the CSRS. The person managing the CSRS presents a detailed scenario that contains incidents that relate to the issues being explored. The incidents are designed to create a response from at least two of the personae so that interdependence develops among them. In general, when an incident arises, the members who share that persona must discuss and negotiate whether and how they should respond. This may create a need for further research to support the feasibility of the action and provide details of such action. Responses may be initiated via telephone, computer-mediated communication and/or face-to-face meetings. During these interactions various personae may collaborate to share tasks, roles and resources to achieve common goals. The CSRS manager may release new incidents during this phase that will change the pattern and direction of the interactions between personae. This can be used to help ensure the learning outcomes from the activity are achieved. This phase comprises most of the interaction between individuals and among groups as the players respond to events and each other's actions.

A *forum event* is constructed around a public forum. It follows a formal agenda to support the personae reaching decisions on various issues. This event may use various communication media depending on the geographic location of participants. Position papers may be required prior to the forum and these may be used to supplement the verbal or written interaction that occurs during the forum. The forum can play an important role in creating closure for the persona-related interactions between the participants and for the individual personae.

During the *reflection phase* participants identify what they have learned as a consequence of participating in the events of the CSRS. Normally this occurs as a verbal debriefing following a structured process involving guided recall, reflection and analysis of the experience. This facilitates systematic self-reflection, intensification and personalization of the experience followed by generalization and application of learning from the experience (Lederman, 1992). Where the goal of the CSRS is to understand multiple perspectives relating to an issue it is important to involve participants representing all personae. This debriefing process also encourages participants to jointly construct meaning through small and large group discussion. Individuals' learning outcomes may also be represented via a written paper.

Pollutsim

The computer-supported roleplay-simulation Pollutsim provides a context where learners develop an understanding and insight of issues related to the management of a contaminated site. Pollutsim was first used in 1996 and has been refined in response to evaluation and student feedback. The Pollutsim scenario involves an industrial company, which operates an arsenic-producing smelter. The company-owned vacant land adjacent to the smelter is found to have soil and groundwater contaminated by arsenic and petroleum hydro-carbons, which have the potential to impact on community resources in the area. The scenario is designed to create conflict among the personae on a range of environmental issues.

The learning objectives for Pollutsim are to:

- identify the political, social, economic and scientific dimensions to decision making in an environmental conflict at a contaminated site;
- identify the responsibilities and appropriate responses for characters in the roleplay simulation; and
- develop communication, negotiation and decision-making skills (McLaughlan and Kirkpatrick, 1999).

Learners adopt various personae in the scenario in order to respond to issues and problems that arise as they seek to deal with potentially impacted community resources. The roleplay simulation involves up to 24 personae comprising business, regulatory, political, media and citizen groups. Personae are randomly allocated to participants so there is no matching of discipline area, background knowledge or previous experience. Undergraduate and postgraduate university students studying courses in engineering and various types of resource management have participated in Pollutsim.

During the *briefing* phase, a voluntary two-hour training session was provided to familiarize students with the software used to support the roleplay simulation. To support the development of participants' social skills and promote interaction using computer-mediated communication (CMC), all participants took part in a two-hour online group-based training session. Participants received the scenario prior to the interaction phase. This was to allow them to familiarize themselves with the scenario, identify their persona preference and research their selected persona before events commenced. To encourage ownership of the personae, participants were allowed to self-select roles where possible. Most personae and the site were modelled on real organizations and roles, and a genuine location was used to create an authentic social and cultural perspective for the participants. This also minimized the amount of background material that had to be created for the roleplay simulation. It was necessary for some personae to develop an understanding of technical information relevant to their role.

The *interaction* phase commenced with a face-to-face session based on the proceedings of a public community meeting to discuss the issues raised by the scenario. While the remainder of the roleplay simulation occurred online, the first event occurred in a face-to-face setting in order to establish social relationships and promote interaction. Interaction relating to the roleplay simulation took place in a distributed fashion using CMC over a seven-week period. While some private e-mail was used to communicate between personae, most dialogue was posted to a discussion group (public e-mail) for all personae to access. During the interaction phase the CSRS manager released information on new incidents and provided advice on personae behaviour and options as requested. An anonymous login to the software system was provided for participants to express points of view with which their persona may not have wanted to be publicly associated. This option allowed some relevant issues to be aired. To promote accountability, a self and peer assessment system was used to assess the responses of the personae during this interaction phase.

Pollutsim concluded with a three-hour, public community-style meeting chaired by an appropriate persona whose goal was to identify the extent to which agreement could be reached on issues raised during the interaction phase.

The *reflection* phase involved a face-to-face debriefing immediately after the forum for all participants. During the debriefing participants identified the key factors implicated in environmental decision making. Several weeks after the verbal debriefing, participants submitted individual written papers and concept maps that represented the learning outcomes of Pollutsim.

Successful engagement in the roleplay simulation required students to communicate with each other to negotiate and resolve conflicts relating to the management of a polluted site. Specifically, students needed to be able to perform communication tasks at a range of levels of difficulty appropriate to the particular context in which they occurred. The performance of these tasks required students to act independently or in conjunction with others while the emphasis placed on each task varied according to the role and context.

Middle East Simulation

The Middle East Simulation (MES) was designed for political science (international relations of the Middle East) students in 1993 (Vincent and Shepherd, 1998; Alexander and McKenzie, 1998). The learning objectives for the MES were to:

- introduce students to the facts of Middle East politics;
- give them experience with the complexities of negotiation and decision making in 'real' political systems; and
- improve their skills in using computer technology and the Internet as tools for the workplace (Vincent and Shepherd, 1998).

In our use of MES, participation was extended to include students from an engineering course at another university. This interdisciplinary collaboration was intended to provide an opportunity for engineering and political science students to participate in a collaborative learning activity. It was anticipated that the engineering students would develop an understanding of the interrelationship between technology, culture and politics. The original scenario and the personae were modified to allow interaction between the political science students and the engineering students across a broader range of issues. Additional roles were created to allow greater representation of technologically related personae and a media role controlled by technological personae was created to facilitate information flow within the simulation. Typical political personae involved leaders of countries within the region or stateless political figures. A total of 31 personae were developed including political roles, technological personae (often government ministers, leaders of government organizations or multinational companies) and representatives of the media.

During the *briefing* phase a voluntary training session using the CSRS software was available to students. Students were allocated personae based on their preferences and discipline and then developed relevant role profiles. In addition, the engineering students produced a position paper on either the status of water resources or information technology within the region. To develop sufficient context-specific knowledge to enable them to execute their role, engineering students researched a specific issue related to an incident that would occur within the scenario. The engineering students also received a brief lecture that provided an overview of the politics within the region.

The *interaction* phase began with the release of a scenario and ran for almost four weeks. The scenario included 18 incidents based around a water-resource issue (for example, a drought, an infrastructure project), an information technology issue (for example an infrastructure project, a military application) or political activity (for example, a terrorist attack, a political statement). Each incident was designed to have cultural, political, security, developmental or economic implications and involve particular personae. During the interaction phase different synchronous chat sessions were held for specifically invited personae or for all personae as appropriate. The CSRS rules required all public announcements to be made through the media personae. Only private e-mails between various personae were allowed. This created strong role interdependence between the media and other personae.

The *forum* involved a three-hour face-to-face conference-style meeting. Position papers were developed by political personae prior to the forum and the agenda items for discussion were developed by a political persona who had a mediation role within the MES. Agenda items related to issues that had arisen during the interaction phase of the activity and various personae were invited to speak to each agenda item followed by discussion.

The *reflection* phase comprised an optional verbal debriefing immediately after the conclusion of the forum. Two weeks after the verbal debriefing, engineering students submitted a paper identifying what they believed they had learned and an interaction report detailing how they had contributed to the MES and to their persona. This comprised a journal of the time spent and activities undertaken during MES.

Student responses to CSRS

The two roleplay simulations that we have described provide examples of peer learning activities that occurred in an online environment. In order to complete the learning tasks embedded in the roleplay simulations successfully, students needed to work collaboratively with others who shared their persona and to interact and negotiate with students representing other personae as the events of the roleplay simulation unfolded. It was not possible for students to complete the task without engaging with other students. The roleplay simulations were designed to encourage interaction and engagement with key concepts and issues related to the content of the subject. The inclusion of computer support provided students with additional means of communication and flexibility in relation to the time and place at which communications could occur as well as access to electronic resource materials.

On the whole, students' responses to these experiences have been positive, including comments such as 'the simulation provided a new and very exciting learning experience that is flexible, even to part-time students' and 'this simulation has been the highlight of my university study'.

Student feedback identified a range of positive features associated with the roleplay simulation, the online environment and learning with and from peers. Students reported that the CSRS provided a valuable opportunity to interact with other students, to understand other perspectives on an issue and to become involved actively in the process of learning. They appreciated the opportunity to see the complexities of situations that involved their discipline and they described the experience as providing a different view:

> [As engineers] we're normally not trained to see all of the picture. This made us look at it all. I believe that it gives us [engineering students] a good insight into very different global issues that we do not experience throughout the course of studying an engineering degree.
>
> Having been through the majority of my secondary and tertiary training focusing on the purely technical aspects of technology, I have rarely had the chance to be exposed to the resultant impacts related to introducing a new technology into society. The subject. . . has been as interesting as it was helpful to the development of my professional engineering skills. Although many people have been aware that numerous issues did exist, not much has previously been done in terms of educating engineering students about this topic.

Students perceived that the CSRS helped them to develop a broader view of their discipline and broadened their understanding:

> My experience with this simulation has given me a whole new perspective to think about when trying to resolve a problem. Sometimes other factors must be taken into consideration, factors such as cultural, social, political, and technological issues
>
> The Middle East Simulation has definitely been worthwhile, since it allowed my team and myself to engage in a role interacting with people from various different fields, experience the reactions and decisions that other people made based on our professional opinions.

Students who participated in the MES commented on the value of learning about how different subject experts approach the problem: 'it's a powerful way of learning about other people's perspectives – what they are and how to work with them'.

However, different levels of subject knowledge influenced how well students from the two courses worked together:

> Interacting with the [other course] students was difficult as we did not have the political background needed to anticipate events in the simulation in the correct manner. Although the [other course] students appreciated our point of view on many issues, they also noted that we acted inappropriately in many situations and made it difficult for them to complete their policy objectives.

There is an obvious tension that arises as a consequence of bringing together students from different disciplines to work together. As in the real world there is a need to balance alternate perspectives with knowledge and understanding of the discipline area. While previous comments demonstrate that many students appreciated the diversity of opinion and expertise, others perceived this as restricting communication:

> On one side there were students from a very technical and scientific background, the other were students from a very political and social background. This, I perceived, was one of the major factors contributing to the communication barrier.

Students highlighted the power of learning from each other, and the need to develop the skills that would allow them to identify and draw on the expertise of others. They recognized the applicability of this to the world of work beyond university:

> I benefited from this simulation in many ways as I practised my communication skills, got to understand the current Middle East crisis, interact with political people and most important improved my negotiation skills. In general, I am pleased with this simulation because it added a lot to my interpersonal skills and opened my mind to a different world.

The novel nature of the roleplay-simulation and working in the online environment motivated students to engage in the activity. Students appreciated the flexibility associated with communicating and working online. As with all forms of collaborative work where students are required to work with others there were issues associated with the difficulty of getting together and the problems relating to the development of a climate of trust and effective communication. To a large extent the use of the online environment overcame the inconveniences normally associated with working together on a task. It also made it possible for students from distant geographic locations to work together and share information:

> Communication between group members was easy to control as we made full use of the diary, e-mail and phone facilities available to us. By using these information/communication sources, decisions took into account the ideas and views of the entire group. In that way, conflict was avoided as all members were kept well informed and we were all participating in the whole process.

In this context, students recognized that additional time was required to organize themselves as a group:

> Just the fact that we needed to always collaborate took a lot of organizing and time away from other activities. However student commitments and time obviously limit the amount of simulation interaction and organization of our team.

A common student criticism of group work activities is the presence of 'freeloaders', those team members who contribute little to the group. This was not widespread in the two CSRS cases, although it was reported in the MES where students perceived that group members from the 'other' university course did not always contribute to the work of the group. Generally, students felt that the workload was shared equally among members of their persona team:

> The workload was equally shared amongst our group throughout the entire simulation.

> Our group was able to work effectively together. We all understood what was required and as such we came to expect this in each other.

We hope that this is a direct consequence of the design of the scenarios and processes that were intended to promote equitable responsibility and effort:

> No direct conflict occurred within our group throughout the simulation period. While our team members obviously brought to the group different background values and beliefs, we worked well together in establishing the direction our character would take in the simulation.

Another aid to our cohesive team was our familiarity with each other. So we were aware of each other's strengths and weakness, unlike many of the other groups, which had experienced a 'breaking in' period where the members got to know each other.

Sharing personae seems to provide an additional layer to the challenges of working together on something like a roleplay simulation, which is time consuming and demanding in any circumstance:

As there are three members in our team who tried to cooperate as one character, this has caused some conflict in the process of decision making and negotiation strategies.

I found it even harder when three members. . . from different cultures and beliefs tried to play the same character. This caused some conflicts while we implemented our negotiation strategies and carried out our objectives.

Some difficulties related to characteristics of individual students whilst others related to communicating with each other and generally arose as a consequence of technical difficulties or incompatibility:

There was no conflict between members as such, but communication was hindered due to the availability and time constraints of each member. These constraints prevented members from logging on at the same time, and also to contact each other for advice and discussions.

It was easier when we negotiated face to face before sending a formal letter via e-mail to confirm our 'interests'.

Issues

The simulations encouraged students to work together in a collaborative manner. While there may have been aspects of the individual scenarios that required personae to behave in ways that were competitive, within this students shared knowledge and skills as necessary to resolve the scenario. Within the MES, the scenario focused on incidents that involved either water resource or information technology issues. It was intended that engineering and political science students would need to collaborate in order to deal with these incidents. The relatively low level of knowledge about technology-related issues by the political science students and poor knowledge of the politics of the region by the engineering students created a requirement for significant sharing of understandings to develop appropriate political actions that were technologically feasible.

There were particular issues associated with cross-institutional involvement in the CSRS. In the main these related to different expectations of teaching staff from each course and consequent different student expectations and behaviours. However we believe the value of students learning with and from students from other discipline areas and from other institutional cultures outweighs the problems we encountered, many of which may be resolved through clearer communications between teaching staff.

Roleplay simulations can create high levels of interdependence among learners as they work together in a common enterprise. Where students from diverse discipline backgrounds bring a variety of expectations and priorities it is essential that different learning outcomes and assessment practices are closely aligned. Assessment practices have a significant influence on where students focus their attention. Within Pollutsim, all students, despite their different backgrounds, worked within the same assessment regime. Thus, all participants were being assessed on similar learning outcomes for the roleplay/simulation. This meant that it was likely that students shared an understanding about what was considered important and there was a perception of equitable assessment and workload among participants.

Within the MES, the political science and engineering students were expected to achieve significantly different learning outcomes and were assessed using different techniques and tasks. Although the scenario was designed to create interdependence, the differing learning outcomes created a degree of independence between the student groups. For political science students the MES was not portrayed as central to developing the knowledge required for the subject, rather it was a means of displaying their knowledge. However, in the case of the engineering students, the knowledge generated during the MES was the basis for understanding interrelationships between technology, politics and culture. Students were expected to learn about these as consequence of participating in the MES. This fundamental difference in the desired learning outcomes and assumptions about how they would be achieved resulted in different emphases in relation to expectations about assessment of student learning. The reflection phase, particularly the verbal debriefing, was considered an essential part of the learning process for the engineering students, but this phase was not essential for political science students and did not contribute to their assessment.

Designers and participants of CSRS must identify the communication media that will most effectively support the specific communication needs associated with different tasks. Designers must ensure that all necessary media are available and participants need to be able to use these effectively to achieve their desired purpose. Participants also need communication and group work skills that will allow them to function effectively in traditional face-to-face settings and in a computer-mediated environment. Our experiences to date show that face-to-face meetings are essential at particular stages of a roleplay simulation. Student feedback reinforces our observation that the need for face-to-face communication occurs during the initial stages of the collaborative experience (interaction phase) when both group formation and a shared understanding of the problem are being developed, and in the reflection/synthesis phase. During other phases of the experience computer-mediated communication provides adequate support for learner interactions.

The use of the online learning environment exerts additional pressure for learners to have effective group work and communication skills especially in relation to using new media. However, learning through CSRS can also provide support for the structured development of such skills.

Conclusion

Our experiences in the two CSRS described earlier in this chapter provide support for the use of online environments to facilitate collaborative learning among geographically and temporally distributed learners. Online technologies, specifically CMC, open up opportunities for learners to interact and collaborate in ways that may be different from more familiar face-to-face interactions but which nevertheless develop the conditions necessary for collaborative and peer learning. We believe that the traditional conventions that apply to collaborative work are relevant in the online environment and that roleplay simulations create the conditions necessary for peer learning to occur. We believe that CSRS effectively maintain the promotive interaction necessary for individuals and groups to work in a way that is truly collaborative rather than simply distributed individual effort.

References

Alexander, S and McKenzie, J (1998) *An evaluation of information technology projects*, Committee for University Teaching and Staff Development and Department of Employment, Education and Youth Affairs, Canberra
Errington, E (1997) *Role Play*, HERDSA Green Guide No 21, HERDSA, Canberra

Lederman, L (1992) Debriefing: towards a systematic assessment of theory and practice, *Simulation & Gaming*, **23** (2), pp 145–60

McLaughlan, R and Kirkpatrick, D (1998) *Developing a Framework for Effective Electronically Supported Simulations.* Paper presented to the annual Higher Education Research Development Society of Australasia Conference (HERDSA), Auckland, New Zealand, July, http://www.auckland.ac.nz/cpd/HERDSA/HTML/TchLearn/Mclau_Ki.HTM

McLaughlan, R and Kirkpatrick, D (1999 A decision making simulation using computer mediated communication, *Australian Journal of Educational Technology,* **15** (3), pp 242–56: http://cleo.murdoch.edu.au/ajet/ajet15/mclaughlan.html

Vincent, A and Shepherd, J (1998) Experiences in teaching Middle East politics via Internet-based role-play simulations, *Journal of Interactive Media in Education*, **98**, p 11, http://www-jime.open.ac.uk/98/11/vincent-98-11-paper.html

11

Aligning peer assessment with peer learning for large classes: the case for an online self and peer assessment system

Mark Freeman and Jo McKenzie

Very large classes provide challenges for lecturers and students. Loss of individual contact between teachers and students and student feelings of anonymity give rise to a series of possible problems. For students, these can include lack of understanding of subject goals, lack of individual feedback on learning, lack of opportunities for discussion with others and the feeling that the subject is impersonal. For lecturers, issues include difficulties in knowing what students are really learning, inability to get to know students, difficulty in providing individualized feedback, challenges in dealing with student diversity and problems in engaging students in learning (Biggs, 1999; Davis and McLeod, 1996; Gibbs and Jenkins, 1992). In this environment, peer learning offers potential for improving students' learning, developing their teamwork capabilities and helping them to develop a greater sense of connectedness to others. However, implementation of peer learning in large classes raises particular challenges, such as providing feedback on teamwork, controlling student 'free riding' and developing multiple tutors' and lecturers' capacity to engage with peer learning processes.

The objective of this chapter is to describe a range of peer learning approaches that have been used in face-to-face and online classes to encourage higher quality student learning in a large first-year undergraduate business subject. A key strategy has been the linking of peer learning with peer assessment using an online confidential system for self and peer assessment of teamwork. The chapter should interest those wishing to use peer learning in large classes and/or use self and peer assessment of teamwork. In the chapter, we describe the steps taken to incorporate peer learning in business finance, what was learned about successful implementation and the challenges for subject coordinators and lecturers.

Integrating peer learning into the teaching and learning environment

Business finance has been a first-year core subject in the Bachelor of Business at the University of Technology, Sydney (UTS) for many years. It has seven objectives relating to various graduate attributes desirable in a business professional. Some of these relate to students knowing or being able to apply technical material. Others relate to generic attributes like the ability to work in a diverse team and to use technology effectively.

A decade ago the subject had 260 on-campus students studying at one campus and was taught by two to three full-time staff. Contact time for each student was a one-hour large lecture followed by an interactive two-hour tutorial with rarely more than 20 students in the class. In the last five years, business finance has had up to 1,000 students per semester and is taught in parallel at two campuses. Reduced funding per student means that contact time for each student comprises a two-hour mass lecture plus a one-hour workshop with over 40 students. One full-time lecturer coordinates the subject and delivers all of the lectures by travelling between campuses. As many as 13 part-time lecturers are involved in giving workshops. The student group is considerably more diverse with eight times the number of overseas students than were enrolled ten years ago.

A variety of teaching and learning activities and resources are used to encourage students to learn in the subject: lectures and workshops, printed lecture workbooks, interactive online learning activities, a CD-ROM containing self-managed learning materials and a team case study assignment. Some have impact on student grades and others have a formative feedback purpose. The following sections focus on those that incorporate peer learning.

Peer learning in face-to-face classes

Efforts to integrate peer learning in face-to-face classes have yielded both successful and less-than-successful outcomes. The major success has been achieved in the two-hour lectures run by the subject coordinator. These lectures have up to 400 students in typical tiered lecture theatres. Students come to the lecture with a workbook incorporating the key points of the lecture along with examples and practice problems from past exams. Students work on the practice problems in pairs at regular intervals, as related concepts are introduced. From time to time, they explain difficult concepts to each other. This enables students to experience differences in meaning, assist each other's understanding, identify areas where they are having difficulty and gain immediate and focused feedback on learning. In introducing the activities, the lecturer stresses the value of students learning from each other and the benefits that students are likely to gain by participating. Student feedback indicated that students valued these opportunities very highly in this subject, but many other business subjects underuse them.

The opportunities for peer learning designed for the tutorials, now rebadged as 'workshops', were less successful. In business finance these are intended to go beyond the traditional tutorial format where a tutor directs and encourages discussion. Model solutions to practise 'homework' problems are made available to students in advance. Students are encouraged to work through the problems with a friend and to use the model answers to self-assess their progress so that new problems can be introduced during workshops for students to complete in groups. The workshop lecturer is then meant to draw out the learning from the new group problems.

Feedback from workshop lecturers indicates that the potential for peer learning in the workshops is not realized, for a variety of reasons. Many workshop lecturers, often inexperienced part-time teachers, have found the one-hour time frame, class size and diversity of the student group pose real dilemmas. Workshops typically contain 40 students, of whom half are international students of various nationalities. Language differences mean that students can have difficulty understanding each other and familiar anecdotes from one culture cannot be relied on to help peers from other cultural backgrounds to connect new concepts with prior experiences or under-standings. More time is needed for reading and speaking. Also, many students, whether international or local, initially expect a teacher-focused environment inside the classroom, although they may be used to engaging in peer learning outside the classroom (Biggs, 1999; Tang, 1993, 1998). Many workshop lecturers reported conflicts between their desire to use the peer learning activities and students' expectations. The lecturers' experience was that students 'demand' to be led through the model answers to all the homework problems and that this subsumes the time set aside for the new peer learning activities. The challenge for workshop lecturers may be to convince students of the value of peer learning, but this is only possible if the lecturers are themselves convinced that peer learning will achieve better outcomes.

Peer learning using educational technologies

Almost 90 per cent of business finance students have off-campus access to the Internet, and this increased student access to technology has enabled the integration of further peer learning activities into the subject (Freeman, 1996, 1998). In 1997, a university-wide decision to support an online course management and learning system combined with the strategic initiative of flexible learning meant online peer learning activities became both possible and necessary. Various online learning tasks were designed to replace some face-to-face contact. In business finance, students were provided with optional self-assessment opportunities, including sets of questions with automatic feedback provided online and/or on CD-ROM. Because these tasks aimed to provide formative feedback and have no assessment weighting, students were encouraged to do them in pairs to gain the benefits of learning from each other. Students responded very positively (Freeman, 1997). Some students not only learned about the subject but also learned skills in using computers or accessing the Internet.

Students also used threaded discussions to pose questions that could be answered by their peers or by the lecturer. The discussion threads are visible throughout the semester, so other students can follow student interactions. Peer learning by lurking in these discussion forums is qualitatively different to peer learning by listening in a face-to-face classroom, in part because students have more time to read, think and reflect on what they are reading. Students rated highly the opportunity to learn business finance from their peers through online discussions, even when they never contributed to them (Freeman, 1997). Further research identified a significantly greater appreciation for this form of peer learning by students from non-English-speaking backgrounds. Another interesting twist came in the years when an anonymous login was provided. We observed past students voluntarily answering some of the posted questions. Observing informal peer tutoring online was very satisfying.

More complex peer learning tasks have also been developed in other subjects containing an online element. Asynchronous team-based debates and anonymous asynchronous role-play simulations (Freeman and Capper, 1999) are just two. They encourage reflection, research and opportunities for peer learning not easily achievable through face-to-face or print media.

In summary, a range of face-to-face and online peer learning activities have been used to encourage student learning. The majority included formative feedback. But not all students have chosen to participate. Peer learning has been strongly encouraged by the lecturer but it has mostly been optional for students, with some strongly perceiving its value and others working individually. The next section describes the ways in which peer learning and self and peer assessment have been linked in a compulsory assessable task that encourages students to develop their capacity for teamwork.

Aligning peer learning with peer assessment

Formal assessment is the final method for integrating peer learning in business finance. Students take many of their cues for learning from assessment. As Ramsden (1992: 187) comments, 'from our students' point of view, assessment always defines the actual curriculum'. The Oxford Centre for Staff and Learning Development (1997) maintains that teachers often confuse two broad purposes of assessment. Formative assessment should be frequent to motivate students, provide feedback on their strengths and weaknesses, and provide feedback to staff on student progress. Summative assessment should be much less frequent but more rigorous because it aims to certify the quality of student learning and achievement of the subject objectives (Biggs, 1999) and be a quality assurance measure. The assessment in business finance was developed with this in mind.

The overall assessment package comprises a set of learning tasks that students must pass, a team-based case study and a final examination. These attempt to align student effort to achieve seven subject objectives, of which the ability to work in a team is one. Each assessment task is criterion referenced and model answers are provided where possible. The weighting for the tasks is reflected below.

Weight	Assessment task
Pass/fail	Completion of various learning tasks (for example CD-ROM, online quizzes, study guide)
35%	Three-part team-based case study
65%	Final exam (20 multiple choice and 4 multi-part problems)
100%	

Students are encouraged to work with a peer on the pass/fail learning tasks. While the current assessment package has zero weighting for this aspect, sometimes it has been worth up to 10 per cent on completion (for example, the average of the best three out of five online quizzes). To ensure a focus on learning, students can choose to submit online tasks multiple times. It is explained to students that they although they are not prevented from putting in another student's answers (cheating) or putting in a random submission, they would be unwise to do so because the weighted assessment tasks have similar problems or build on knowledge developed through these learning tasks.

These tasks and some of the peer learning tasks done in class or as homework are explicitly related to the highly weighted final exam, which covers all content of the subject. It aims to test students' ability to recall key information, apply simple and complex procedures to new problems, interpret results and evaluate alternative approaches. To discourage reliance on rote learning, it is a limited open-book examination. The criteria to be assessed are explicitly articulated and students can compare the reality with the rhetoric by viewing past exam papers that are made available online with model answers and marking scales.

The case study aims to achieve several generic attributes, in particular the ability to work in a team, the ability to communicate, an ability to use technology (spreadsheets, word processors and the World Wide Web) and the ability to apply key disciplinary techniques. It became a team task in 1993 when teamworking capability was included in the subject objectives, and is now done each semester by up to 330 teams containing between three and five members. It is submitted in three parts over the semester to encourage ongoing application of newly introduced content and to provide feedback on understanding well before the final submission date. The context of the case study is as relevant to the 'real world' as possible. Students must analyse ambiguous information, predict the future, develop a business plan, justify the link between numbers and theory, articulate how they would deal with managers that may not be cognizant with the benefits of current techniques, and work with colleagues from different cultures and with different priorities.

In feedback surveys and focus groups, students have frequently commented on the value of this case study assessment task as a learning activity. But when it became a team task, students vehemently complained about the problem of some members not pulling their weight – the so-called free rider or social loafing effect (Latane, Williams and Harkins, 1979; Michaelsen, Watson, Craigin and Fink, 1982). Peer assessment had been successfully applied in the summative assessment of a team project in another subject (Freeman, 1995). In the process, the subject coordinator learned about using self and peer assessment to adjust group marks to reflect the perceived contributions of individual team members. It was decided to experiment with this alternative approach for the team case study.

There were two main purposes for introducing self and peer assessment of teamwork in the case study task. Firstly, it is a way of enhancing individual students' awareness of the different task and team process roles necessary for successful teamwork, and the individual contributions that they make to the team's success. Secondly, it tries to make team assessment fairer for students by moderating the team marks to better reflect individuals' contributions. It was also important that any procedure would not be too burdensome for staff, which was easily possible with over 300 teams. Initial experiments relied on teams submitting a sheet with the final part of their case study where the team gave an aggregate weighting of each individual's effort to the team assessment task. All students would sign off that they were happy with these aggregate weightings. A student who received a 100 per cent weighting would then receive the team project mark, whereas a student who received 90 per cent weighting would get 90 per cent of the mark. This approach did not reduce the level of angst caused by free riders, evident from the number of teams requiring dispute resolution and the high reference to this issue in student feedback surveys. Variations of this approach were equally unsuccessful. The desire to resolve this issue and improve students' learning about teamwork led to the development of a confidential online system. A prototype version of the system was tested in business finance in 1996 and 1997, leading to an application for a National Teaching Development Grant for funding for SPARK, a fully functioning Web-based system. The following section describes the system and its implementation and evaluation.

SPARK: a confidential online system for self and peer assessment

SPARK stands for Self and Peer Assessment Resource Kit. It enables students to rate their own and each other's contributions to different aspects of a team task, using multiple assessment criteria. The student ratings are then combined to produce a self and peer assessment factor used to moderate the team mark for each individual team member. The program can be used with any class size and has been tested in a variety of discipline areas as well as business. It is based on educational research, in particular that put forward by Goldfinch (1994), and differs from the aggregate weighting approach in four significant ways:

- The adjustment factor is an average of a range of individual criteria. This should result in a more accurate assessment of each member as a variety of aspects of the team project and process can be considered.
- The adjustment factor is calculated from each individual student's ratings of themselves and each of their peers, rather than being a weighting agreed by the whole group.

- Submissions by each team member are confidential. This should encourage honesty and greater integrity in the outcome.
- The data can be aggregated in other ways to provide formative feedback.

In business finance, the primary focus for using SPARK has been on adjusting the team case study mark to reflect students' individual contributions to teamwork. The process used in implementing SPARK is as follows:

1. The team assessment task is designed and communicated to students. Issues like how teams are formed, what the assessment task is, how it will be introduced, what criteria will be used to assess the task and the individuals' contributions to the team, how these criteria align to subject objectives and so on must be addressed. In particular, it is essential to use appropriate criteria for students to assess their own and their peers' contributions to the team. Criteria can be pre-set by lecturers, or negotiated by lecturers and students together. The latter is highly desirable so that students feel a sense of ownership of the criteria, but it can prove difficult in very large classes. In business finance, the lecturer used a process half-way between these options. In the first year in which the prototype of SPARK was used (1996) a focus group of previous students provided feedback on their own experiences. The students identified eleven activities undertaken during the group case study which could be used as criteria to prompt students' memories of their contributions. These covered a range of categories including 'task leadership', 'number crunching' and 'writing the report'. The group was then asked to comment on the items that might be used in the final calculation of the self and peer assessment factor. These mostly related to the attributes of an effectively functioning group. The resultant final criteria were: 'level of enthusiasm and participation', 'brainstorming ideas', 'gathering and analysing research', 'helping the group to function well as a team', 'organizing the team and ensuring things got done' and 'performing tasks efficiently'. The first few times self and peer assessment were used, students were asked to comment on the appropriateness of the criteria. They have been seen as reasonable and thus have remained largely unchanged.
2. Students, teams, team registration and assessment dates and the assessment criteria are entered into the SPARK system. Students may register their own teams, or the lecturer can choose teams in advance. Students require a password to enter the system, reducing the likelihood of misuse. Once all of this information is entered, students can gain access to the system at any time. They are encouraged to familiarize themselves with the self and peer assessment criteria and discuss them in their team, deciding

how to allocate or share roles and tasks. The effect of self and peer assessment on adjusting the team-based case study mark is explained to students. Students can also simulate different levels or types of contribution (via a spreadsheet) to see the effect on their grade. Feedback from surveys indicates that students appreciate the provision of explicit criteria. They can see that their development of generic attributes (for example the ability to work in a team) will be assessed. In this way we have attempted to align student perceptions with the actual alignment of objectives, teaching and learning activities and assessment.

3. Students undertake the team assessment task. Upon submission they then rate their own contributions and their team peers on a confidential basis. The ratings are submitted online during the allocated period, typically several days to a week. They may be changed by resubmission at any time during that period. While doing the task, students are encouraged to retain a diary of activities to prompt their subsequent ratings at the end of the subject. The diaries are also useful in the event of team disputes.

4. The teacher requests SPARK to calculate the various self and peer assessment factors at the conclusion of the rating period. The self and peer assessment (SPA) adjustment factor is calculated as follows: SPA adjustment factor = v (total ratings for an individual)/(average of total for each individual). The results can then be exported to a file (or transposed manually). If SPARK is used for summative purposes, the lecturer typically imports the SPA factors into a spreadsheet to adjust the team mark into an individual mark for each student.

Obtaining an individual mark for a team or group project: example of SPARK output

Table 10.1 shows examples of what the self and peer ratings and adjustment factors could look like for a team task scoring 25. The examples assume a rating scale where '0' equates to no contribution, '1' to below average for that team, '2' to average for that team and '3' as above average for that team. The average ratings are compiled automatically from the multiple criteria used by each student. Team A members perceived that they contributed equally, so each individual in Team A ends up with a factor of 1 ($\sqrt{8}/8$) and therefore the same mark for the team task. In contrast, Team B perceived that David contribute less than average ($\sqrt{5}/8 = 0.79 = 0.8$ below) and this is reflected in his lower individual mark. They perceive that Celine contributed more

Table 11.1

TEAM A	Average rating for student . . .			
	Ang	Belinda	Chong	Jose
Rated by student				
Ang	2	2	2	2
Belinda	2	2	2	2
Chong	2	2	2	2
Jose	2	2	2	2
Total	8	8	8	8
SPA factor	1.0	1.0	1.0	1.0
Team mark	25	25	25	25
Individual mark	25	25	25	25

TEAM B	Average rating for student . . .			
	Amy	Bob	Celine	David
Rated by student				
Ana	2	2	3	1
Bob	2	2	3	1
Celine	2	2	2	1
David	2	2	3	2
Total	8	8	11	5
SPA factor	1.0	1.0	1.2	0.8
Team mark	25	25	25	25
Individual mark	25	25	29	20

than the average (ie $\sqrt{11}/8 = 1.17 = 1.2$ above) and this is reflected in her higher individual mark (ie $1.17 \times 25 = 29$ above). To retain confidentiality, students are not given their team's actual spreadsheet.

SPARK can also be used for formative feedback, even prior to completion of an assessment task. This is achieved by comparing the average peer ratings to the self-rating. Since David's average self-assessment factor (in Team B) is higher (at 2) than his peers' assessment of his abilities and/or efforts (at average of 1), David has overrated his contribution compared with his peers. David can be made aware that he needs to increase his efforts or work on his team skills. In contrast, Celine has underestimated her efforts or ability to work in a team. She needs to be encouraged about her positive contribution. For more detailed formative feedback, teachers could also provide students with a profile of how their peers had collectively rated them on each of the criteria. Students can be encouraged to use this as the basis for discussion to confirm that their team is working well or renegotiate team contributions.

Effects of using SPARK

Students in business finance (and other subjects) have provided positive feedback on the use of SPARK. The team assessment process is perceived by most students to be fairer due to confidentiality, the explicit use of multiple criteria, the ability to revisit one's ratings multiple times and the knowledge that contributions to the team will be rewarded and free riders will be penalized. Students can see the alignment of assessment to subject objectives that relate to teamwork skill development. The number of complaints about the team aspect of the case study has reduced substantially. With over 300 teams it is not surprising that the problem has not gone away altogether. But because students can play with the demonstration spreadsheet and evaluate the effect of not contributing, there is a reduced likelihood of the problem occurring.

The disadvantages to students relate to the extra layer of technology and the inherent risks of relying on it. Some students have been anxious that their ratings may not be submitted (even though the system provides an electronic receipt) or that other students may discover their ratings. The latter problem is not unique to SPARK. There is also the equity issue and lecturers have to be sensitive to the needs of the 10 per cent of students who don't have off-campus Internet access. Some students, particularly those with a highly competitive attitude, have commented that the system is open to abuse as students can intentionally overrate themselves and underrate their peers to gain a competitive advantage. While there is little evidence of this, it can happen and points to the need for teachers to maintain a 'hands-on' approach to using the system and being accessible to resolve problems.

The benefits to staff relate mainly to satisfaction and time saving. Lecturer satisfaction is a major benefit as the lecturer perceives that the process is a fair way of identifying individuals' contributions and that it encourages the achievement of multiple subject objectives. Using SPARK for data collection, data entry, data validation and calculation has made this complex process of self and peer assessment less time consuming than the less effective paper based method used previously. Even having a computer say 'you cannot have a team in excess of five members' helps save time arguing the not-so-special cases that business finance students previously put forward.

Reactions have been mixed at the departmental level. Some colleagues have sought to use SPARK for managing self and peer assessment to encourage student contributions to assessed team tasks in their subjects but found it did not work. In several cases this occurred because they did not choose appropriate criteria for their assessment task. Positive experiences by colleagues in other faculties that use SPARK for summative assessment are more the norm. Interestingly, it was a colleague who chose to use SPARK for formative feedback that brought this use to our attention.

While SPARK has been useful for self and peer assessment, how does it relate to peer learning? We believe that it can encourage more effective peer learning in teams for several reasons. Because the criteria are explicit and accessible from the time that the task is commenced, students have a clear framework for negotiation about how their teams will function. It is more obvious that students can make equal but different contributions. This can raise students' awareness of the value of the differences that each individual brings to the team and encourage them to learn from each other's strengths. In feedback surveys, around half of the students consistently report that the system had helped them to learn more about the different aspects of teamwork and had made them aware of aspects of teamwork that they had not previously considered. Using the system formatively, in a constructive peer learning context, can help students to learn more about their own contributions and how these are perceived by their peers. All of these points are possible without the use of a system like SPARK. However, we have found that the explicitness and relative anonymity that the system provides are important in using self and peer assessment in very large classes where the possibilities for individual teacher advice are much more limited.

Ideally to gain the maximum benefits from peer learning as compared with assessment, the system would allow student teams to negotiate the criteria that they thought were important and would allow for these criteria to vary between teams, perhaps with some non-negotiables set by the teacher. This is possible with the current system, but it is administratively difficult and further enhancements may provide this functionality.

Conclusion

As this chapter has illustrated, peer learning has considerable potential for engaging students in effective learning in very large classes but, even more than usual, its success depends on convincing other staff and students of its value. For some lecturers and tutors, using peer learning effectively depends on them changing their conception of teaching towards one of student-focused facilitation of learning (Prosser and Trigwell, 1999). Lecturers whose conceptions of teaching are limited to transmission of information may not see students as legitimate contributors to their peers' learning, and this can lead some to see peer learning as a form of cheating. Clearly we would seek to discourage this view and convince our colleagues of the benefits of peer learning.

Some students may need convincing too. Those who view teachers as the legitimate source of authorized knowledge (Baxter-Magolda, 1992; Perry, 1999) may initially view peer learning as a way for the teacher to abandon large numbers of students or avoid work. Those who are particularly competitive may be reluctant to help their peers learn. Ironically, the role of the teacher in encouraging students to see the benefits of peer learning cannot be underestimated, particularly in large classes where feelings of anonymity seem to encourage some students to act in excessively competitive, individualistic or even unethical ways. In these classes, actively encouraging peer learning and helping students to experience the benefits can go a long way towards improving the learning environment for both students and teachers.

Peer assessment does not necessarily mean peer learning or vice versa, but it is possible to use them together in complementary ways. SPARK is one attempt to align peer assessment with peer learning while managing student perceptions of the fairness of team assessment in very large classes. It can be used to reward peer learning effort and/or provide feedback on the development of students' teamwork capabilities. But we have learned from experience that it is not an automated solution that enables teachers to set teamwork and leave students alone to get on with it. Class time still needs to be devoted to developing students' abilities to work in a team and discussing task and team process roles. Criteria need to be carefully designed, preferably in negotiation with students as part of class teamwork discussions. Teachers still need to monitor the progress of student groups and be on hand to mediate disagreements.

At a societal level we need to be doing something to develop the graduate attribute of teamwork, encourage and value collaboration and maximize the contributions that students can make to each other's learning. There are several ways to encourage peer learning and teamwork in both traditional and more flexible learning environments. The development of the online confidential self and peer assessment system is producing positive responses in Australia and Europe. The success of our efforts ultimately depends on the appreciation by teachers and students of the real benefits of peer learning and teamwork.

References

Baxter-Magolda, M (1992) *Knowing and Reasoning in College: Gender related patterns in students' intellectual development*, Jossey-Bass, San Francisco

Biggs, J (1999) *Teaching for Quality Learning at University*, SRHE and Open University Press, Buckingham

Davis, G and McLeod, N (1996) Teaching large classes: the silver lining, *HERDSA News*, **18** (1), pp 3–5, 20

Freeman, M (1995) Peer assessment by groups of group work, *Assessment and Evaluation in Higher Education*, **20** (3), pp 295–306

Freeman, M (1996) The role of the Internet in teaching large undergraduate classes, *Flexible Online Learning Journal*, **1** (1), http://www.lib.uts.edu.au/folp/journal/index.html

Freeman, M (1997) Flexibility in access, interaction and assessment: the case for web based conferencing and teaching programs, *Australian Journal of Educational Technology*, **13** (1), pp 23–29, http://cleo.murdoch.edu.au/gen/aset/ajet/ajet13/wi97p23.html

Freeman, M and Capper, J (1999) Exploiting the Web for education: an anonymous asynchronous role simulation, *Australian Journal of Educational Technology*, **15** (1), pp 95–116, http://cleo.murdoch.edu.au/ajet/ajet15/freeman.html

Gibbs, G and Jenkins, A (eds) (1992) *Teaching Large Classes in Higher Education*, Kogan Page, London

Goldfinch, J (1994) Further developments in peer assessment of group projects, *Assessment and Evaluation in Higher Education*, **19** (1), pp 29–35

Latane, B, Williams, K and Harkins, S (1979) Many hands make light work: the cause and consequences of social loafing, *Journal of Personality and Social Psychology*, **37**, pp 822–32

Michaelsen, L, Watson, W, Craigin, J and Fink, L (1982) Team learning: a potential solution to the problems of large classes, *The Organisational Behaviour Teaching Journal*, **7** (1), pp 13–22

Oxford Centre for Staff and Learning Development (1997) Oxford Brookes University, http://www.brookes.ac.uk/services/ocsd/aup14pr.html

Perry, W (1999) *Forms of Ethical and Intellectual Development in the College Years: A scheme*, Jossey-Bass, San Francisco

Prosser, M and Trigwell, K (1999) *Understanding Teaching and Learning: The experience in higher education*, SRHE and Open University Press, Buckingham

Ramsden, P (1992) *Learning to Teach in Higher Education*, Routledge, London

Tang, C (1993) Spontaneous collaborative learning: a new dimension in student learning experience? *Higher Education Research and Development News*, **12**, pp 115–30

Tang, C (1998) Effect of collaborative learning on the quality of assessments, in (eds) B Dart and G Boulton-Lewis *Teaching and Learning in Higher Education*, Australian Council for Educational Research, Camberwell, Victoria

12

Conclusion: challenges and new directions

David Boud

Previous chapters have introduced the ideas behind peer learning in university courses, have considered the ways in which it can be used, and have given examples of many different peer learning practices. The experiences of the various practitioners who have implemented these practices demonstrate that there are difficult issues to be addressed and that there are important considerations to be worked through for anyone contemplating using such approaches.

The aim of this concluding chapter is to reflect the main issues, identify the challenges these represent and explore some of the directions peer learning might take. We emphasize the importance of thinking of university courses in terms of how high-quality teaching and learning environments can be constructed and sustained rather than in terms of just the teaching of subject matter. We suggest that consideration of peer learning is central to the construction of such environments. In thinking of the future, we acknowledge the pressures higher education is currently facing and may continue to face.

We end by noting key questions about how as peers we can learn from those we do not identify as teachers. We believe that the ways in which such questions are addressed as part of university courses are pivotal to the development of peer learning and central to the construction of high-quality learning environments. The future development of peer learning is not a matter of developing new strategies but of changing conceptions about what it means to learn in higher education.

Issues emerging

We have seen in this book that peer learning must respond to the actual circumstances of a particular course. There are no quick-fix strategies that will be effective in all circumstances. As we have seen in the variety of approaches used by different authors, there are as many ways of using peer learning as there are courses being offered. What works with small classes, for example, needs to be modified for large ones, and the reverse also applies. What is effective in one discipline area will not necessarily work in another with different teaching and learning traditions and different expectations about what students will learn. We need a large repertoire of strategies to draw upon and we need to know how to adapt these to fit our own needs.

Our contributors have also illustrated the irony of peer learning requiring teachers to make it effective. Teaching staff need to be well prepared and to understand the dynamics of teaching and learning. The larger the class, the greater the care that needs to be taken in establishing an appropriate strategy and ensuring that students fully understand what is involved. This also requires that a sufficient and compelling rationale be given for students to want to engage in it and persist in overcoming the inevitable difficulties they will encounter. As we have also seen in the chapters discussing the challenges of large classes, staff need to be convinced that peer learning will lead to good learning outcomes. This is a significant issue when there are teams of staff involved. Unconvinced and disorganized members of a team can undermine the most carefully laid plans.

It is interesting to note that almost all of the case studies in the second section of the book show that it is necessary to undertake a number of iterations to enable peer learning activities to work well in any given setting. The first cycle of implementation often throws up as many problems as it solves. Because of the need to fit strategies to the circumstances of each class, the process cannot be guaranteed to be highly effective first time around. Teachers need to learn a lot about the processes involved and how to tailor them for any given group. Most importantly, it is necessary to enter into the use of peer learning with the expectation that several cycles will be needed before it can fully deliver the outcomes it promises.

The discussions about group assessment in Chapters 6 to 11 highlight students' great sensitivity about fairness. They resent 'free riders' and do not want them rewarded for exploiting the work of others. While students are unlikely to want to expose them directly, they do want assessment systems that ensure others do not benefit when they have not made a contribution to the group. A peer learning activity will only be acceptable to students if they regard it as equitable. Peer assessment has an important contribution to make to peer learning activities but it needs to be especially carefully designed to avoid it having the opposite effect to what is intended and disrupt desirable collaboration between peers. Perceived lack of fairness is likely to be the single greatest factor undermining implementation of peer learning strategies.

Changes to secondary schooling mean that students now have far more experience of working cooperatively with others than ever before. However, despite these changes many contributors report that students entering higher education do not have the skills to enable them to work readily with each other. Students can and do react negatively to group work when it is poorly organized and if they are not equipped to use it well. Learning about how groups operate, how learning can be facilitated and how to give each other feedback are not just interesting options but may need to be incorporated as normal parts of the curriculum, as we have seen. Time spent on these activities does not necessarily detract from the pursuit of other content goals, but is often an excellent investment leading to more effective and long-term learning.

The difficulties faced in large classes with a very mixed student population were illustrated well in Chapter 7. The prospect of working in highly diverse groups, or groups with students from other cultures, may be seen by some students as inhibiting their learning of subject matter, because of the need to invest time and effort into working with peers who may not share their assumptions. The longer-term learning outcomes and benefits of being able to work well with a diversity of colleagues needs to be sold to many students and this goal made legitimate as a normal part of a course. The rhetoric of the benefits of diversity needs to be translated into concrete practices that students feel to be of benefit to them. It is only through placing considerable effort in pursuing this goal that it will be possible to ensure that all students benefit from peer learning, not just those who need it the least and can organize it without assistance.

While it may not be immediately apparent from the preceding chapters because all the contributors share a common view on it, the use of peer learning assumes a learner-centred perspective. Such a perspective places the learner, rather than the subject matter to be taught, as the central feature in course design. Holding such a view does not imply any lesser commitment to a discipline, but it does mean that disciplinary and professional concerns are necessarily mediated by acceptance of a primary responsibility to the students actually enrolled in a course. It is easy to claim a learner-centred perspective but the translation of the claim into practice requires a good appreciation of who the students are, what their aspirations are and some knowledge of how students learn in higher education. Some of the problems in the use of peer learning arise from a lack of appreciation of the student experience and an unwillingness to take sufficiently seriously the difficulties learners have in coping with the course as it has been constructed. Just because the process works well for highly motivated and well-prepared students, does not mean that it is at all suitable for those who may not have the same background and commitments. Adoption of peer learning requires that staff listen carefully to students and modify their practices to address the issues which emerge.

The last two chapters demonstrate ways in which new technologies have created new opportunities for peer learning. They show that online learning does more than provide a convenient forum for students who may not otherwise be able to meet each other. It allows for different learning outcomes to be pursued. It provides for ways of managing processes of interaction and keeping track of assessment in ways students can see to be fair. Web-based technologies provide a range of opportunities the potential of which is only recently being explored. They need to be deployed to ensure that all students are engaged, not just those who can see the immediate benefit for themselves. It is likely that we will see much more innovation with regard to peer learning and new technologies in the next few years.

The various contributors to this book have noted in many places the constraints that limitations on resources are placing on university courses. Much of the innovation described here was prompted by the need to address problems created by increased student numbers or larger class sizes. The pressures on higher education have never been greater and the threats to quality never higher. What was commonplace in a three-year undergraduate degree can no longer be sustained without a substantial injection of resources. We are unlikely to see such an injection to support all students and all courses. There will continue to be downward pressures on resources for teaching and learning. The danger is that ill-considered solutions will be promoted and they will be taken seriously. Already online learning – although holding enormous promise – has been substantially over-hyped as a solution to problems it cannot possibly address by those who should know better.

A final observation on the preceding chapters is that all the examples discussed previously involve strong integration between peer learning and the other teaching and learning activities used in the course. While it may have originally been picked up as a useful addition to the programme, it has ended up as a key element of the overall design. It is usefully seen as an element of course design that complements other activities.

The construction of high-quality learning environments

Recognition of the integrated nature of teaching and learning represents for us a shift of emphasis in thinking about the use of peer learning in university courses. Peer learning activities *per se* are not important – what matters is their contribution to the overall learning experience of students. The examples we have seen are a significant addition to the quality of courses. In many cases they have transformed the nature of students' experience.

An engagement with peer learning, as we have seen in this book, directs attention to changes in thinking about the design and conduct of courses. If we adopt a learner-centred approach, as we have accepted we need to do, then we need to think about course design as the construction of high-quality learning environments. Students operate in these learning environments to pursue the goals of a course. While these environments may include various contributions by teaching staff, they are not driven by staff in the ways that traditional lecture courses are driven by what occurs in lectures.

The components of these learning environments would include sets of course materials, meetings between staff and students, assessment tasks and peer learning activities, but the mix of these might be radically different according to the learning outcomes desired. In some programmes substantial individual assessment tasks might drive the work of students, in others the focus might be on collective products. In all the emphasis is on what students do. What staff do is irrelevant except insofar as it impinges directly on the nature of the learning activities in which students engage.

In such environments, the bulk of staff attention before the start is given to the design and structure of the total set of activities, on the resources provided and the affordances accompanying these resources and on the structuring of the tasks in which students are to be engaged. During a course, attention is given to equipping students to benefit from the facilities provided, to fine tuning activities in the light of actual reactions and to ensuring that students are learning the kinds of things which the environment has been set up to promote and portraying them appropriately. Following the course, attention is given to learning what it is that has been effective in the environment provided and what needs to be changed to make it more so.

This is no different to what most of the authors of the chapters have been describing as their practice, but it is framing it differently. It is a radically different framing to that which has been used in the past to describe most courses. In this new framing, all events and activities are subordinated to the goal of students' learning. It is what students do that is foregrounded. What teachers do is no less important, but it is not foregrounded in the way it is with lecture courses. Staff are not defined by their qualities as teachers or lecturers, but in terms of their ability to construct and maintain high-quality learning environments.

Staff roles are already shifting rapidly. They are not just managers of learning, though they are that also. They are not just monitors of quality assurance, though they must do that too. They provide the vision for what is to be learned. They provide the enthusiasm to encourage students to persist in the hard work of learning. They orchestrate the programme to make it happen, and they intervene thoughtfully (and in a limited way) to ensure that learners set themselves sufficiently demanding expectations and bring about a sense of accomplishment. They do this in the context of particular subject matter and in a particular context.

When we see courses in this way, it is no longer meaningful to think of peer learning as a separate element. It is an obvious and necessary element of all environments and attention must be given to it as much as to the preparation of resources or the structuring of assessment tasks.

Key challenges for peer learning

We believe that the use of peer learning can be considerably enhanced by attention to the issues identified earlier and by viewing peer learning from the perspective of high-quality learning environments, but there are more fundamental issues to be addressed. These are not simply matters of design and implementation but lie at the heart of our educational culture. They require substantial attention not only because they are significant for peer learning and higher education generally, but also because they influence learning in the changing societies of the twenty-first century.

They can be expressed as 'how do we learn from someone we don't know?' and the complementary question, 'how do we learn from those with whom we do not identify?' These are not questions asked in earlier times. We would simply not have thought to ask them. They were not significant at a time when we had extensive contact with teachers and other students, when we experienced continuity in learning over time. Neither were they significant when we had enough exposure to teachers and other students to develop relationships that enabled us to identify what they had to offer and decide whether we should take them seriously.

We have seen in the examples in Chapters 6 and 7 the problems that occur when there is a high, and unfamiliar, level of diversity in groups. Students often do not believe that other students, different from themselves, can contribute much to their learning. These other students may come from different cultural backgrounds, may not be native English speakers or may be different in other ways. When the focus of learning is on the immediate subject matter, anything providing an immediate barrier to communication can be used as an excuse for lack of engagement. When these other students are not seen as part of the future with which it will be necessary to engage, an important incentive to work through the differences is missing.

To foster peer learning in circumstances where there is the anonymity of large and diverse groups requires a focus on learning outcomes beyond those related to the immediate subject matter. Learning to learn from each other must be a legitimate goal for the overall course if peer learning is to be accepted. It must be an explicit part of the normal course and justified as important as other outcomes. Learning to work in a team must turn into an immediate goal for the here and now, not just a general aspiration for a degree programme.

It is not just unfamiliarity with others that acts as a barrier. There are sometimes more negative dynamics at work. As we discussed in Chapter 2, there is unhelpful baggage that learners bring to any situation and that interferes with their own learning as well as that of others. Both from their own personal histories and from the influence of wider social pressures, students act oppressively to each other and may even act in ways that are directly discriminatory. Very rarely is this oppression or discrimination anything to do with the actual people who are interacting with each other. Neither is it to do with the material being studied. Nevertheless, there is a great responsibility for teaching staff to address the problems created because this baggage gets directly in the way of learning and engagement with the subject.

While there may be oppressive acts, and students may not realize what the effects of their behaviour is on others, there is still potential for students to learn from and with each other. They need to learn ways of overcoming these negative dynamics. It is not easy. Learning involves being willing to be open to the ideas of others. Openness requires us to trust the other party. Trust is fostered by disclosure – disclosure begets disclosure – and preparedness to take risks. Unless this cycle is entered, learning is hard to achieve. The obligation is on staff to enter the cycle and model the kinds of disclosure and risk-taking that are needed to confront the negative behaviour. This is not a new challenge, but peer learning highlights the importance of the intervention.

We open ourselves up to others when we recognize something of ourselves in them, when we can identify with them. Without this identification, the steps that need to be taken along the path of trust will not be taken. We know more about peer learning when we learn more about how we respond to others and extend the range of our own responses when we notice that what we are doing has a positive or negative influence on others.

The challenge for the designers of learning environments is to lower the threshold of tolerance for others. That is, to make the process of learning with and from each other as important an outcome as the subject-related objectives. The challenge is to construct an environment in which risk-taking and self-disclosure can take place, in which working with diversity is the norm not the exception and in which learning is the *raison d'être*. There is no technological fix for this. Indeed, some of the possibilities which technology provides adds to the complexity of the challenge. However, the experience of working with the fragmented possibilities of Web-based learning also means that students are more prepared to set aside some of their assumptions about ways of interacting with others and deal with the learning environment we create on its merits.

Peer learning will grow whether or not books like this foster it. There is little alternative if higher education is to pursue a wide range of educational goals and equip students for an unknown future. It is ironic though that a practice celebrated in stories of students in elite institutions as a way of coping with the expectations of academics there is finding itself as a key strategy in enabling the mainstream of institutions to cope with circumstances beyond their control.

The challenge of peer learning is not to make it foolproof. It will always be demanding for students and it will confront them with difficulties they will need to address. Some unnecessary difficulties can be eliminated by well-designed activities. However, it is only when students encounter and engage seriously with the issues it highlights that they begin to realize the learning outcomes it promotes. Learning with and from each other is not easy; learning how to do this is a central outcome of higher education.

Author index

Subject index

CPSIA information can be obtained at www.ICGtesting.com
Printed in the USA
LVOW13s0621100814

397886LV00015B/106/P